SSAT/ISEE (Upper) Vocabulary:
1500 words testing Synonyms/ Antonyms/ Homophones/ Idioms/ Blanks

In 10 minute Vocabulary tests

By

J Christine

How to use this book

This book tests over 1500 words that frequently appear in the SSAT/ISEE Upper Examination.

There are 50 sets containing 28 questions each.

Each set should be done in 10 minutes.

Try to set aside a period of 30-60 minutes each day and do one or two tests.

Short periods of regular study are more effective than long irregular sessions.

Make a note of the questions you get wrong, and revise them with the help of the answers given at the end of this book.

To learn new words;

- Study the definition, part of speech and example sentences with the help of a dictionary.
- Practice saying the word aloud.
- Some students find it helps to copy out the words in a notebook to learn the spelling.
- If you have a study partner try to explain to him/her what the word means.
- Try to write your own example sentence using the new word.

Tips for taking the tests

- Since the tests are timed, you should <u>not</u> spend too much time on any one question.

- Ensure that you read the instructions carefully, e.g. sometimes students may confuse an antonym question for a synonym one, and select incorrect answers for the whole section!

- <u>After the test</u>, make sure that you learn ALL the words in the tests and not just the ones that a question may be asking for specifically.

  e.g. If you are asked to find the <u>synonym</u> for **venerate,** you may already know that the correct answer is **revere**. Don't stop here but ensure that you also learn the meanings of <u>all</u> the other answer choices while revising the test. (*pontificate, lacerate, sublimate and anticipate*).

  The words used are the ones that commonly appear in the SSAT/ISEE tests so being familiar with more of them will result in a higher score.

- For the *'Fill in blanks type'* questions, you may need to skip a question if you get stuck, but come back to it after reading more of the text. This will provide further context/clues that may enable you to now answer the question.

Note: In the unlikely case that you find any typos/errata in this book, kindly let us know at;
expresseducationlimited@gmail.com
You will receive a surprise gift along with a note of thanks from us!

V0.1

Tests

Sets 1 - 50

Set 1

A. Synonyms

Select the word that most closely matches the meaning of the word provided.

1. **meek**	ecstatic	quiet	boisterous	empty	heartfelt
2. **immure**	incarcerate	hunt	kill	emancipate	torture
3. **wily**	ridiculous	cunning	lavish	extreme	slimy
4. **venerate**	pontificate	lacerate	sublimate	anticipate	revere
5. **esoteric**	unwitting	factual	crude	fortunate	abstruse
6. **adamant**	loose	omnipotent	determined	sluggish	peaceful
7. **callous**	passionate	heartless	fast	immense	impeccable
8. **corrosive**	touching	gaunt	lowly	destructive	lighthearted

B. Fill in the blanks

Fill in the blanks from the words in the table below. There are two extra words you do not need.

frugal	amicable	detest	limber	avert	barter	confer

1. The poor artist would often _____ his drawings for a meal.

2. Although I like most foods, I _____ red meat.

3. The family spent a lot of money. They said they had to be _____ for the rest of the month.

4. The movie was so scary, most of the class had to _____ their eyes.

5. The board had some issues last month; everyone is hoping this month's meeting will be more

   _____.

C. Homophones and homographs

Homophones are two or more words having the same pronunciation but different spellings and meanings. Homographs are words which have the same spelling but different meanings.

From the list below, fill in the blanks. (The first one has been done for you).

shore	sure	stair	stare	minute	frequent

1. To be certain of something   _____sure_____

2. The area of land before the sea   _____

3. To often visit a place   _____

4. A step   _____

5. Something that is done often   _____

6. To be extremely small   _____

7. A part of an hour   _____

8. To gaze at someone or something   _____

D. Synonyms - Spelling

Complete the synonym of the word in **bold**.

1. **forge**   s __ __ p e

2. **proud**   s m __ __

3. **peruse**   s c r u __ __ __ l z e

4. **stoical**   p __ t i __ __ t

5. **funny**   j o __ __ l a r

6. **consolidate** c o __ __ l n e

7. **deprave**   c o r __ __ p t

Set 2

A. Synonyms

Select the word that most closely matches the meaning of the word provided.

1. **affluent**   discreet   desolate   rich   shiny   delightful

2. **animosity**   touching   opposition   tiresome   extinct   telling

3. **unsystematic**   cunning   haphazard   mischievous   mindful   smelly

4. **languid**   <u>slow</u>   appetizing   free   emotional   amicable

5. **chagrin**   still   appeased   loud   scared   annoyance

6. **chide**   berate   recommend   confer   sell   take

7. **cataclysmic**   violent   point   misplace   explain   pardon

8. **rectitude**   pulled   integrity   disagree   destruct   correct

B. Missing words

Choose the best word to complete the sentences.

There are a (1) _____ (multitude, multi, multitudes) of hobbies to participate in. These days, (2) _____ (stranger, bizarre, bizare) hobbies are becoming more popular than before. One interesting hobby to mention is extreme ironing. People have taken to ironing in the most (3) _____ (formidable, formadable, fermidible) locations. These include cliff edges, and even under the water! People who take part in this hobby are often tired of (4) _____ (exciting, tedious, hardwearing) day-to-day tasks. Either way, this hobby is not for the (5) _____ (brave, bold, fainthearted).

C. Antonyms

Pick the word that means the opposite or near opposite of the word provided.

1.	**mediocre**	tarnish	fooled	free	loose	special
2.	**repulse**	tighten	peel	praise	welcome	repel
3.	**vice**	forgive	provide	please	grab	virtue
4.	**vex**	appease	anger	prepare	battle	tire
5.	**palpable**	intangible	coincide	fight	abhorrent	make
6.	**pariah**	anathema	member	outcast	teacher	adult
7.	**obviate**	allow	forestall	destroy	speak	find
8.	**overt**	belittle	cherish	conceal	plain	mild

D. Idioms

Match each idiom to its meaning.

1.	**Blow off steam**	a. Do well at something (usually after practicing)
2.	**Raining cats and dogs**	b. Raining heavily
3.	**In a pickle**	c. Dislike something a lot
4.	**Get the hang of it**	d. Inability to cope with a situation
5.	**All over the show**	e. Do something to relax
6.	**Can't hack it**	f. Complete mess
7.	**Break a leg**	g. Wish good luck (usually said to someone in a performance)

Set 3

A. Synonyms

Select the word that most closely matches the meaning of the word provided.

1. **admonish**   assemble   burn   toil   treat   warn

2. **frenetic**   energetic   arrogant   lethargic   gnarly   posthumous

3. **acrimonious**   bitter   outlandish   heady   fantastic   mild

4. **acclaim**   support   organize   praise   practice   laugh

5. **tarry**   shout   loiter   experiment   lie   solve

6. **efface**   tussle   trip   mind   eradicate   taste

7. **muddle**   jostle   hack   confuse   berate   fold

8. **thwart**   trial   bead   glide   obtain   obstruct

B. Fill in the blanks

Fill in the blanks from the words in the table below. There are two extra words you do not need.

atone	meander	pristine	aspire	viscous	erratic	desiccate

1. The item being sold online had never been used. The seller said it was in _____ condition.

2. His behavior recently has been quite _____.

3. In spring, I like to _____ through woods and forests.

4. The syrup was _____ and it was fun to watch it drip off the spoon.

5. The students in the drama class have a lot in common. They all _____ to be famous film

actors and actresses.

C. Homophones and homographs

Homophones are two or more words having the same pronunciation but different spellings and meanings. Homographs are words which have the same spelling but different meanings.

From the list below, fill in the blanks.

birth	berth	hall	blue	haul	May

1.   The fifth month of the year   _____

2.   A color   _____

3.   A large room used for meetings or events   _____

4.   The start of life   _____

5.   To pull something with effort   _____

6.   To feel in a low mood   _____

7.   A word used to give permission   _____

8.   A place at a dock for a ship   _____

D. Synonyms - Spelling

Complete the synonym of the word in **bold**.

1. **brazen**   b o __ __

2. **candor**   h o __ __ s t y

3. **boorish**   r __ __ e

4. **mettle**   n __ __ v e

5. **prognosis**   d i a g __ __ s i s

6. **stoical**   c __ __ l

7. **prudent**   c a __ __ f u l

Set 4

A. Synonyms

Select the word that most closely matches the meaning of the word provided.

1.	**stamina**	finite	fiendish	endurance	telling	fruitful
2.	**shun**	reject	elicit	ignite	weave	crush
3.	**inexorable**	divulge	finance	obdurate	digress	obsess
4.	**rabid**	sad	mad	mild	loud	light
5.	**quotidian**	tepid	truthful	passive	ordinary	needed
6.	**voluble**	frantic	ultimate	garrulous	bizarre	fanciful
7.	**yoke**	abolish	emancipate	fill	grant	tyranny
8.	**vituperate**	vilify	uphold	agree	combine	misery

B. Missing words

Choose the best word to complete the sentences.

The honeybee is most likely the most (1)_____ (beautifully, wonderfully, commonly) known bees in the world. Honeybees have a complicated community and (2) _____ (purchase, produce, find) honey that is enjoyed across the globe. There are different (3) _____ (bees, workers, roles) within the honeybee community. The queen is the (4) _____ (leg, head, arm) of the community and is usually the largest honeybee in the hive. She has a (5) _____ (crucial, impossible, ordinary) job within the hive.

C. Antonyms

Pick the word that means the opposite or near opposite of the word provided.

1.	**wistful**	drive	bold	pathetic	hideous	joyful
2.	**zealous**	depressed	apathetic	soft	appealing	exasperated
3.	**expunge**	foretell	confirm	pack	delete	elate
4.	**didactic**	educational	brash	preachy	corrupting	instructive
5.	**duress**	panic	prude	freedom	wise	mettle
6.	**deluge**	golden	arid	poor	wet	flavorful
7.	**detract**	hop	jostle	nip	enhance	sell
8.	**devious**	baffle	battle	dark	prank	fair

D. Idioms

Match each idiom to its meaning.

1. **A blessing in disguise**   a. To have two good situations

2. **Spill the beans**   b. To tell someone something (usually tell a secret)

3. **Takes two to tango**   c. Get something done you don't want to do

4. **Bite the bullet**   d. To have something good happen from a bad situation

5. **Cutting corners**   e. Agree with someone

6. **You can say that again**   f. Both parties are equally responsible for a situation or an argument

7. **The best of both worlds**   g. To do something the easiest or cheapest way

Set 5

A. Synonyms

Select the word that most closely matches the meaning of the word provided.

1.	**dexterity**	avarice	skill	soiled	bonny	glutinous
2.	**diatribe**	eloquent	embezzle	extol	insular	tirade
3.	**cubicle**	booth	demure	postcard	ambush	dessert
4.	**bellow**	lament	praise	shout	finalize	ambush
5.	**cusp**	maintain	edge	tabletop	turnip	vial
6.	**amiss**	censure	mound	ambivalent	wrong	demur
7.	**refute**	approve	disprove	lace	bend	flick
8.	**anthology**	map	crossword	collection	illness	selfish

B. Fill in the blanks

Fill in the blanks from the words in the table below. There are two extra words you do not need.

raze	lanky	recoil	expiate	prologue	prudent	hardy

1. People with no experience looking after plants are recommended to buy a plant that is _____.

2. The scene of the horror film was so gruesome; she could not help but _____.

3. Whilst in court, the robber had the chance to _____ his crimes.

4. The only way to rebuild this place is to _____ it first.

5. The text had an extremely interesting _____ that the whole class enjoyed reading.

C. Homophones and homographs

Homophones are two or more words having the same pronunciation but different spellings and meanings. Homographs are words which have the same spelling but different meanings.

From the list below, fill in the blanks.

bank	letter	weigh	principle	principal	way

1.   The head of a school   _____

2.   The side of a river   _____

3.   To have weight   _____

4.   A rule   _____

5.   A place to keep money   _____

6.   Part of the alphabet   _____

7.   A plan or a method   _____

8.   A written note   _____

D. Synonyms - Spelling

Complete the synonym of the word in **bold**.

1. **debris**   t __ __ s h

2. **wily**   c u __ __ i n g

3. **vitriolic**   h o s __ __ l e

4. **nomadic**   w a __ __ e r i n g

5. **nascent**   b u __ __ i n g

6. **denizen**   r e __ __ d e n t

7. **apex**   p __ __ k

Set 6

A. Synonyms

Select the word that most closely matches the meaning of the word provided.

1.	**annihilate**	pick up	fall out	wipe out	bolt up	scatter
2.	**ardor**	passion	light	lamp	obliterate	creep
3.	**benign**	harmful	help out	free	harmless	assort
4.	**brisk**	quick	slow	beautiful	cruel	peachy
5.	**covet**	height	desire	pick	stupor	uneasy
5.	**embark**	loop	erase	pile	begin	consume
6.	**epoch**	fighter	period	hearsay	yearly	jester
7.	**quibble**	savor	knit	kneel	elaborate	bicker

B. Missing words

Choose the best word to complete the sentences.

William Shakespeare is one of the most (1) _____ (noteble, notable, noble) playwrights in the English-speaking world. He was born in Stratford-upon-Avon in England in 1564. During his life, Shakespeare wrote a (2) _____ (knighted, bright, copious) amount of works, including plays and (3) _____ (rows, poems, magazines). Although Shakespeare died many years ago, his (4) _____ (legacy, children, wife) still lives on in the form of his (5) _____ (house, gardens, works) which are studied and enjoyed by an array of people across the world.

C. Antonyms

Pick the word that means the opposite or near opposite of the word provided.

1.	**lethargy**	languor	lassitude	finite	alacrity	synergy
2.	**protean**	breezy	finding	juiced	pathetic	constant
3.	**puerile**	mature	kibble	excuse	oversight	produce
4.	**languish**	ingest	fade	flourish	fight	strive
5.	**lax**	loaded	tight	bruised	teach	clear
6.	**ennui**	contentment	kingdom	command	energy	boredom
7.	**envoy**	emissary	delegate	agent	receiver	create
8.	**ameliorate**	disguise	aggravate	indescribable	prove	electrify

D. Idioms

Match each idiom to its meaning.

1.	**A picture is worth a 1000 words**	a. Be very happy
2.	**Put something on ice**	b. Permanently end a relationship/friendship
3.	**As right as rain**	c. Delay something
4.	**Like riding a bicycle**	d. No matter what the situation
5.	**Burn bridges**	e. A skill once learned is never forgotten
6.	**Come rain or shine**	f. Showing something has more value than describing it
7.	**On cloud nine**	g. Feeling well/healthy

Set 7

A. Synonyms

Select the word that most closely matches the meaning of the word provided.

1.	**abrogate**	drought	brought	revoke	bleak	midwinter
2.	**zeal**	junk	jeer	enthusiasm	arrogance	haughty
3.	**solvent**	solution	glutinous	dazed	prolonged	dessert
4.	**impede**	close	dynamic	eloped	pining	prevent
5.	**zephyr**	breeze	wild	nuptial	pride	violated
6.	**deride**	ride	fond	extreme	loosen	ridicule
7.	**stance**	taupe	foliage	posture	beacon	flap
8.	**implore**	plead	please	applaud	plank	piece

B. Fill in the blanks

Fill in the blanks from the words in the table below. There are two extra words you do not need.

desultory	crescendo	assuage	voracious	urbane	vapid	tyro

1. The show had a lot of complaints for being extremely _____.

2. She was extremely polite and _____.

3. The employees were disappointed in their manager's _____ attempt at providing clarity.

4. The student had a _____ appetite for learning.

5. The most exciting part of the orchestra was the _____.

C. Homophones and homographs

Homophones are two or more words having the same pronunciation but different spellings and meanings. Homographs are words which have the same spelling but different meanings.

From the list below, fill in the blanks.

resume	dew	nail	sweet	due	suite

1.   A document showing your work history   _____

2.   The hard part at the end of a finger   _____

3.   Tiny water droplets   _____

4.   Pleasant or agreeable   _____

5.   A place in a hotel   _____

6.   An item used by builders   _____

7.   To start again   _____

8.   Expected at a particular time   _____

D. Synonyms - Spelling

Complete the synonym of the word in **bold**.

1. **torpid**   l e __ __ a r g i c

2. **veneer**   c o __ __ r

3. **ostentatious**   g r __ __ d

4. **sully**   t __ __ n t

5. **plunder**   l __ __ t

6. **portent**   w a r __ i n __

7. **belittle**   d i __ i __ i s h

Set 8

A. Synonyms

Select the word that most closely matches the meaning of the word provided.

1.	**fortify**	pardon	spook	abide	reinforce	squash
2.	**whet**	sharpen	quash	went	wade	creak
3.	**yen**	hate	prune	obstruct	delude	desire
4.	**gauche**	clumsy	bashful	lavish	obscene	neat
5.	**subjugate**	subdue	suppress	survive	sunk	sublime
6.	**vivacious**	lacey	lazy	dead	lively	dwell
7.	**impel**	pricey	edible	fill	urge	connect
8.	**dwindle**	decline	degree	uphold	astonish	jeopardize

B. Missing words

Choose the best word to complete the sentences.

How do you start your day? A cold glass of orange juice? A big bowl of oats? How about a cup of coffee? Coffee is one of the most (1) _____ (hurried, intimidated, popular) drinks to have in the morning in a large number of (2) _____ (countries, countrys, counties). In Vietnam, they have a rather (3) _____ (irrelevant, lardy, unique) coffee: egg coffee! Egg coffee is (4) _____ (traditionally, finally, happily) made with egg yolks, sugar, condensed milk and of course, coffee. What do you think about the sound of egg coffee? Would you give it a (5) _____ (try, make, cup)?

C. Antonyms

Pick the word that means the opposite or near opposite of the word provided.

1.	**gullible**	anthology	garrulous	cynical	incognito	direct
2.	**dulcet**	harsh	sprinkled	decided	gabby	priced
3.	**indecisive**	determined	augmented	free	interviewed	schedule
4.	**sordid**	musically	basically	dirty	respectable	thick
5.	**sporadic**	continuous	daily	monthly	cuddly	intermittent
6.	**gawky**	combined	graceful	conceited	joker	tired
7.	**glut**	scarcity	enrobed	under	lad	golden
8.	**haggard**	haphazard	lax	well	fauna	yen

D. Idioms

Match each idiom to its meaning.

1. **Up in arms** a. Someone who is extremely similar to their mother and/or father

2. **A chip off the old block** b. To become insane

3. **Snowed under** c. Only just

4. **By the skin of your teeth** d. Study with intensity

5. **Lose your marbles** e. Protest vigorously

6. **Hit the books** f. At the beginning again

7. **Back to square one** g. Have a lot of work

Set 9

A. Synonyms

Select the word that most closely matches the meaning of the word provided.

1.	**gilded**	golden	forbade	loose	broken	industrial
2.	**venomous**	poisonous	poised	stumpy	forest	bite
3.	**urban**	city	country	hedgerow	stripe	dune
4.	**vain**	vein	business	conceited	educated	hairdresser
5.	**decrepit**	upstanding	faucet	pine	unfirm	strong
6.	**sustain**	upland	support	plaid	break	clammy
7.	**taboo**	guide	flashy	allowed	woodland	prohibited
8.	**chagrin**	market	assist	trial	annoyance	think

B. Fill in the blanks

Fill in the blanks from the words in the table below. There are two extra words you do not need.

epicurean	accomplice	associate	dialect	contrite	hoodwink	ilk

1. The lecturer and her _____ worked tirelessly researching.

2. The criminal must have had an _____.

3. He knew how to _____ people into giving him money.

4. The feast was extravagant; some would argue it was _____.

5. The professor is an expert at accents and _____s.

C. Homophones and homographs

Homophones are two or more words having the same pronunciation but different spellings and meanings. Homographs are words which have the same spelling but different meanings.

From the list below, fill in the blanks.

whine	down	corps	entrance	core	wine

1.   An alcoholic drink made from grapes   _____

2.   The opposite of exit   _____

3.   A type of feather   _____

4.   The central part   _____

5.   To complain   _____

6.   Part of the army   _____

7.   The opposite of up   _____

8.   To enchant someone   _____

D. Synonyms - Spelling

Complete the synonym of the word in **bold**.

1. **idiosyncrasy**   p e __ __ l i a __ __ t y

2. **illiterate**   u n e __ __ c a t e d

3. **episodic**   o __ __ a s i o n a l

4. **confer**   g i __ __

5. **vex**   a __ n o __

6. **virtuoso**   a __ e __ t

7. **trenchant**   i n __ i s i __ e

Set 10

A. Synonyms

Select the word that most closely matches the meaning of the word provided.

1.	**upbraid**	cutlery	brawn	trying	reproach	rebound
2.	**utilitarian**	useful	positive	head	embezzle	plow
3.	**extirpate**	create	eradicate	dictate	agape	gaze
4.	**clergy**	priesthood	familial	hobby	craft	area
5.	**waif**	unite	finding	telegraph	pupil	ragamuffin
6.	**vulgar**	case	garb	rude	topical	essence
7.	**toady**	frog	sycophant	cultural	beauty	bunch
8.	**toxic**	deadly	vapid	vile	oblong	trunk

B. Missing words

Choose the best word to complete the sentences.

When you think of deadly animals, what springs to mind? Venomous snakes and lions with killer sharp claws? While these are deadly, it is actually the mosquito that is the (1) _____ (deadliest, deadly, dangerousiest) creature in the world. Mosquitoes cause up to a (2) _____ (whooping, whopping, whop) one million deaths every single year across the world.

(3) _____ (Only, Holds, Alone) the female mosquito feeds on the blood of humans, while the male feeds on nectar to stay (4) _____ (live, alive, hungry). Whatever you do during mosquito season, keep a bottle of (5) _____ (water, repellent, sun cream) at hand, and make sure your vaccinations are up to date!

C. Antonyms

Pick the word that means the opposite or near opposite of the word provided.

1.	**theoretical**	practical	foraged	ethical	brutal	resistant
2.	**callous**	arduous	generation	aptitude	kind	intoxicated
3.	**boisterous**	connive	debase	quiet	haughty	insipid
4.	**jocular**	latent	serious	medieval	tremulous	embroil
5.	**gregarious**	bearing	unsociable	credible	zephyr	brine
6.	**detest**	obsess	scoundrel	complacent	hate	love
7.	**aloof**	sociable	nurse	inane	clip	waltz
8.	**pauper**	innate	rags	rich	sauce	hairdo

D. Idioms

Match each idiom to its meaning.

1.	**A short fuse**	a. Reveal a secret by mistake
2.	**Once in a blue moon**	b. Very infrequently
3.	**Cat got your tongue**	c. Start to solve a problem and create havoc
4.	**Put your foot in your mouth**	d. Get involved in something that does not concern you
5.	**Stick your nose in**	e. Say or do something embarrassing
6.	**Let the cat out the bag**	f. Be inexplicably silent
7.	**Open a can of worms**	g. Quick to become ill tempered

Set 11

A. Synonyms

Select the word that most closely matches the meaning of the word provided.

1.	**schism**	solvent	dye	knight	split	smoke
2.	**gradation**	scale	skin	prop-up	confidante	evil
3.	**hardy**	brittle	breakable	fluent	polar	sturdy
4.	**connoisseur**	unknowing	expert	cruel	winemaker	wily
5.	**tenable**	peaky	matte	folded	justifiable	penchant
6.	**brittle**	strobe	hard	jiggly	northern	breakable
7.	**callow**	derelict	rotting	creased	frozen	inexperienced
8.	**cache**	store	bakery	vex	catch	virus

B. Fill in the blanks

Fill in the blanks from the words in the table below. There are two extra words you do not need.

brigand	analogy	placate	resilience	inundate	authentic	perpetuate

1. The designer bag found in the secondhand market was _____.

2. He showed great _____ in the difficult situation.

3. Our teacher used a wonderful _____ to help us understand the new material.

4. The boss tried to _____ the workers with promises and incentives.

5. Despite being on holiday, the manager felt the need to _____ me with messages about the project.

C. Homophones and homographs

Homophones are two or more words having the same pronunciation but different spellings and meanings. Homographs are words which have the same spelling but different meanings.

From the list below, fill in the blanks.

extract	guessed	guest	nose	knows	contract

1. A visitor _____

2. Take out _____

3. A body part _____

4. To get an illness _____

5. He is aware _____

6. A signed agreement _____

7. She didn't know so she did this _____

8. A concentrated solution _____

D. Synonyms - Spelling

Complete the synonym of the word in **bold**.

1. **impartial**   n e __ __ r a l

2. **maker**   c __ __ a t o r

3. **quarrel**   a __ g u m __ n t

4. **meal**   f o __ __

5. **municipality**   d __ __ t r i c t

6. **intoxicated**   d __ u n __

7. **pliable**   f __ e __ __ b l e

Set 12

A. Synonyms

Select the word that most closely matches the meaning of the word provided.

1.	**ire**	kindness	annoyance	brightness	tiredness	fondness
2.	**jargon**	lingo	hunch	proud	collection	ghastly
3.	**jocular**	slice	spatula	pond	polaroid	jolly
4.	**effect**	result	score	point	preview	ore
5.	**mercurial**	healthy	space	erratic	purse	topic
6.	**metropolis**	transport	science	tubular	city	jarred
7.	**cherubic**	treated	robust	philanthropic	ponder	angelic
8.	**citadel**	fountained	fortress	weak	fizzy	skinny

B. Missing words

Choose the best word to complete the sentences.

Have you ever heard of Banksy? Banksy is a (1) _____ (artist, famous, pioneer) artist from England. The identity of Banksy has never been (2) _____ (confirmed, paint, held), but many people enjoy (3) _____ (speculating, lighting, coding) about who he may be. Whoever he may be, his artwork is worth an (4) _____ (large, massive, extortionate) amount of money. His work *Love is in the Bin* sold for over 18 million British Pound Sterling (over 25 million USD) at (5) _____ (auction, sale, house).

C. Antonyms

Pick the word that means the opposite or near opposite of the word provided.

1.	**divulge**	pride	tipple	launch	forage	conceal
2.	**neglect**	abandon	nurture	empathy	admonish	direct
3.	**perennial**	overdevelop	temporary	existing	oversight	moo
4.	**salvage**	destroy	extrapolate	prime	convoy	dire
5.	**opinionated**	similar	indifferent	con	loan	annoying
6.	**unbridled**	restrained	pool	righteous	veal	vanish
7.	**efface**	predispose	create	baffle	cattle	coup
8.	**deadlock**	solution	embellish	warp	bolted	mind-bending

D. Idioms

Match each idiom to its meaning.

1.	**Think big**	a. Have no money
2.	**On point**	b. Have ambition
3.	**Flat broke**	c. Very easy
4.	**Up in the air**	d. Work hard doing long hours
5.	**Burn the midnight oil**	e. Perfect
6.	**Wet behind the ears**	f. Still in the planning stage
7.	**Piece of cake**	g. inexperienced

Set 13

A. Synonyms

Select the word that most closely matches the meaning of the word provided.

1.	**adjourn**	dread	derail	defer	do	journey
2.	**fortify**	strengthen	law	reject	succumb	crumb
3.	**alien**	bay	foreign	whack	scatter	scatterbrain
4.	**feint**	ruse	worth	canker	adore	covet
5.	**expulsion**	array	theory	denizen	banishment	pike
6.	**jeer**	quip	silence	queen	gruesome	claimant
7.	**lucrative**	vegetate	fruitful	bladed	gazed	hone
8.	**terse**	hated	gilded	precise	meandering	spiraled

B. Fill in the blanks

Fill in the blanks from the words in the table below. There are two extra words you do not need.

abridge	adherent	pilfer	rift	semblance	surmount	daunting

1. Once the exams are over, life can return to some _____ of reality.

2. The task was _____ but the brave soldiers decided to take it on.

3. The pickpocket saw the opportunity to _____ a few cents.

4. The company needs to _____ their financial issues in order to survive.

5. He is a strong _____ of the regime, even though it isn't working.

C. Homophones and homographs

Homophones are two or more words having the same pronunciation but different spellings and meanings. Homographs are words which have the same spelling but different meanings.

From the list below, fill in the blanks.

morn	coward	desert	mourn	digest	cowered

1. Process food in the body   _____

2. Someone without courage   _____

3. Literary term for morning   _____

4. A collection of information   _____

5. Fell sorrow after someone's death   _____

6. Abandon   _____

7. Bended in fear   _____

8. A dry place   _____

D. Synonyms - Spelling

Complete the synonym of the word in **bold**.

1. **catalyst**   s __ __ m u __ a n t

2. **incorrigible**   i n c __ __ __ b l e

3. **latent**   v __ __ l e d

4. **confident**   a __ __ e r __ __ v e

5. **nonsense**   d __ __ v e l

6. **rebut**   r e __ __ t e

7. **reprimand**   r __ __ u k e

Set 14

A. Synonyms

Select the word that most closely matches the meaning of the word provided.

1.	**servitude**	subjugation	woe	purify	oxidize	zeal
2.	**slapdash**	organize	nest	trapeze	prattle	haphazard
3.	**stagnant**	inactive	debunk	refute	active	tattoo
4.	**defray**	bankrupt	slaughter	fund	vestibule	coup
5.	**hamper**	stampede	centipede	millipede	impede	retrocede
6.	**hew**	cut	fodder	treaty	singe	abrasive
7.	**doleful**	brazen	afflicted	demolish	abolish	act
8.	**ghostly**	bashful	shaded	eerie	buzzed	goal

B. Missing words

Choose the best word to complete the sentences.

The Red Maple tree is one of the most common trees in the USA and is often found in other countries.

It grows up to 40-60 feet when (1)_____(taken, place, cultivated), but can reach

heights of up to 100 feet when left in the (2)_____(nature, wild, natural). The tree

(3)_____(obscures, prefers, like) soils that are on the

(4)_____(acidic, destructive, aesthetic) side, but is actually extremely

(5)_____(observant, ignorant, tolerant) of a range of soil types.

C. Antonyms

Pick the word that means the opposite or near opposite of the word provided.

1.	**impoverished**	congratulate	connect	jest	wealthy	synthesize
2.	**intricate**	simple	partake	hedonistic	insouciant	jockey
3.	**prim**	foreseen	informal	formidable	trickle	trice
4.	**lucid**	unclear	clawed	impalpable	halo	crusty
5.	**sardonic**	keeper	mushy	polite	cajole	guzzle
6.	**superfluous**	confidential	factual	mutual	existential	essential
7.	**avow**	pry	naught	deny	elderberry	jostle
8.	**taunt**	gnarly	oblique	alkaline	applaud	ostracized

D. Idioms

Match each idiom to its meaning.

1. **Call it a day**   a. Accept too much work

2. **Cat nap**   b. Quit something

3. **Cut someone some slack**   c. Out of control

4. **Get out of hand**   d. Share your thoughts

5. **Get bent out of shape**   e. Don't be overly critical

6. **A penny for your thoughts**   f. Become upset

7. **Bite off more than you can chew**   g. A short sleep

Set 15

A. Synonyms

Select the word that most closely matches the meaning of the word provided.

1. **pensive**   thoughtful   justifiable   destitute   deafening   devastating

2. **perilous**   swamped   disobeying   dangerous   packed   thrilled

3. **shoddy**   horrific   miraculous   inferior   absurd   excellent

4. **sprightly**   bilious   vital   jittery   impeccable   agile

5. **surly**   dour   surely   hour   cower   power

6. **dilate**   enlarge   saunter   scorch   govern   snarl

7. **vagrant**   antic   dowdy   inventive   transient   wretched

8. **assurance**   quarrel   guarantee   hide   oath   rampart

B. Fill in the blanks

Fill in the blanks from the words in the table below. There are two extra words you do not need.

dross	dwindle	flippant	immunity	institute	liability	pugnacious

1. After being exposed to the virus for so long, the community built up a herd _____.

2. A _____ remark made by one of the students infuriated the teacher.

3. The movie's low ratings showed how _____ it was.

4. The doctor trained at the medical _____ for over five years.

5. He became _____ when asked inconvenient questions by the press.

C. Homophones and homographs

Homophones are two or more words having the same pronunciation but different spellings and meanings. Homographs are words which have the same spelling but different meanings.

From the list below, fill in the blanks.

agape	weave	moan	axes	we've	mown

1.   Selfless affection or love   _____

2.   Plural of ax   _____

3.   Contraction of 'we have'   _____

4.   Plural of axis   _____

5.   Join in a pattern   _____

6.   Cut grass   _____

7.   Complain   _____

8.   Wide open   _____

D. Synonyms - Spelling

Complete the synonym of the word in **bold**.

1. **remunerate**   r __ __ m __ u r s e

2. **sparse**   m __ __ g e r

3. **sterling**   e x __ __ l l __ __ t

4. **venture**   r __ __ k

5. **warp**   t __ __ s t

6. **auxiliary**   a __ __ e s s __ r y

7. **candid**   h __ __ e s t

Set 16

A. Synonyms

Select the word that most closely matches the meaning of the word provided.

1.	**drudgery**	stench	clutch	stroll	toil	syntax
2.	**envoy**	delegate	scrawl	bawl	reverberate	jive
3.	**proliferate**	cement	profile	unmade	resonate	breed
4.	**subjugate**	enslave	deprave	stoop	implement	distend
5.	**incinerate**	saunter	burn	gobble	bloat	gravitate
6.	**disentangle**	untwine	revolve	usher	toddle	teeter
7.	**precipice**	castle	tsunami	cloud	sunrise	cliff
8.	**prototype**	put-up	take-up	make-up	dress-up	mock-up

B. Missing words

Choose the best word to complete the sentences.

Do you always wear SPF sunscreen when you go outside? It is (1)_____(non-essential, crutial, paramount) to apply SPF to the skin, due to the

(2)_____(comprehensive, existential, distensibles) protection it provides to

protect against sun-damage. The sun's (3)_____(pernicious, venous, porous) rays

cause issues such as rapid skin ageing and skin cancer. Although it is impossible to

(4)_____(bathe, watch, avoid) the sun altogether, it is possible to reduce sun

(5)_____(exposure, closure, texture) and protect the skin using an SPF sunscreen.

C. Antonyms

Pick the word that means the opposite or near opposite of the word provided.

1.	**pliant**	stiff	conceited	actual	hideous	inverted
2.	**revile**	praise	pray	pardon	plier	persevere
3.	**momentous**	jaw-dropping	ordinary	prime	overt	amicable
4.	**obstreperous**	nebbish	huffed	calm	special	tirade
5.	**perilous**	assisted	enlightened	greeted	safe	itchy
6.	**agitate**	simmer	seethe	smolder	askew	soothe
7.	**erroneous**	middle ground	true	false	coldhearted	complex
8.	**languid**	lethargic	barbaric	toil	active	meddling

D. Idioms

Match each idiom to its meaning.

1. **On top of the world**   a. Enormously proud

2. **Pull one's leg**   b. Be insane

3. **Proud as punch**   c. Make a joke

4. **A bag of tricks**   d. Stay awake all night

5. **Off one's rocker**   e. Extremely happy

6. **Pull an all-nighter**   f. Betray someone

7. **Stab in the back**   g. Techniques, tools and methods used for work

Set 17

A. Synonyms

Select the word that most closely matches the meaning of the word provided.

1.	**exploit**	amuse	abuse	confuse	muse	bruise
2.	**impair**	conjoin	retain	abstain	compile	spoil
3.	**render**	anger	tender	retract	deject	provide
4.	**skeptical**	doubtful	euphoric	impartial	mutinous	piteous
5.	**invincible**	brutal	bulletproof	bonded	bleak	belated
6.	**rugged**	mugged	modular	rough	prized	calamity
7.	**slipshod**	botched	switched	swathed	impeccable	stringent
8.	**extempore**	draconian	gilded	serendipitous	offhand	senile

B. Fill in the blanks

Fill in the blanks from the words in the table below. There are two extra words you do not need.

behave	latent	exquisite	blatant	oblong	polarize	intrepid

1. The crown was decorated with the most _____ stones.

2. There was no need to _____ in a rude manner. The staff were extremely polite.

3. He was naturally _____, even in the most dangerous of situations.

4. The investigators were instructed to search for any _____ fingerprints on the scene.

5. It was _____ that the dog had stolen the treats; there were paw prints everywhere.

C. Homophones and homographs

Homophones are two or more words having the same pronunciation but different spellings and meanings. Homographs are words which have the same spelling but different meanings.

From the list below, fill in the blanks.

chair	coral	latter	coordinate	ladder	choral

1. Something you sit on _____

2. Sung by a choir _____

3. Towards the end of something _____

4. To organize _____

5. Marine life _____

6. Used to locate a position on a map _____

7. A set of steps _____

8. A position of authority _____

D. Synonyms - Spelling

Complete the synonym of the word in **bold**.

1. **abolish**   e__ __ __ i c a t e

2. **venerate**   r e __ __ e __ t

3. **jeer**   m __ __ k

4. **nonplussed**   b__ __ __ s e d

5. **enormity**   i m m e__ __ i t y

6. **real**   a c __ u __ __

7. **unabashed**   __ __ a z e n

Set 18

A. Synonyms

Select the word that most closely matches the meaning of the word provided.

1.	**exculpate**	combine	acquit	paradox	breech	scribble
2.	**forestall**	nuance	thwart	lie	lien	wayside
3.	**garble**	jeep	jump	jingle	jostle	jumble
4.	**proponent**	advocate	longitude	mannerism	quad	longitude
5.	**warble**	trip	force	trill	sluggish	permanent
6.	**recoil**	settle	perfect	modernize	flinch	shove
7.	**relentless**	magnetic	delectable	ruthless	sickly	costly
8.	**rivulet**	gimmicky	gully	golly	mount	trout

B. Missing words

Choose the best word to complete the sentences.

The USA is full of stunning animals and plants, but some species are classed as

(1)_____(innovative, interstrip, invasive) due to the immense

(2)_____(destruction, derelict, delectable) they cause. One species that is considered a

problem is the Giant African Land Snail. The Giant African Land Snail was originally

(3)_____(allow, bring, smuggled) into the USA and has been (4)_____(eloping.

hurrying, causing) issues since. One of the (5)_____(leader, leading, lead) issues is the

parasites they carry.

C. Antonyms

Pick the word that means the opposite or near opposite of the word provided.

1.	**rudimentary**	sophisticated	concrete	working	mysterious	overt
2.	**alacrity**	apathy	covert	apologetic	frightened	insoluble
3.	**flummox**	prohibit	theorize	facilitate	neglect	clarify
4.	**provoke**	lacquer	bash	court	riot	allay
5.	**attest**	bemuse	seclude	veto	increase	stylize
6.	**desperate**	composed	stunted	fooled	betrayed	accustomed
7.	**void**	conglomerate	java	decorate	validate	accelerate
8.	**succeed**	earn	win	fail	yearn	jail

D. Idioms

Match each idiom to its meaning.

1.	**It's not the end of the world**	a. Be successful
2.	**When pigs fly**	b. Very silly, crazy
3.	**Hit the jackpot**	c. In a terrible situation
4.	**As daft as a brush**	d. Never
5.	**Up a creek without a paddle**	e. Be quiet, stop talking
6.	**Raise the roof**	f. Not that bad
7.	**Zip it**	g. Celebrate

Set 19

A. Synonyms

Select the word that most closely matches the meaning of the word provided.

1.	**avuncular**	general	plead	flourished	genial	devious
2.	**bellicose**	aggressive	vehicular	hosted	queer	peculiar
3.	**coax**	rebuke	flatter	castigate	perish	pretend
4.	**boon**	detain	appraise	pact	demand	benefit
5.	**bondage**	theory	repression	azure	adage	elixir
6.	**cant**	impossible	model	hypocrisy	zeitgeist	sequoia
7.	**celerity**	animation	sloppiness	prickles	briskness	celery
8.	**bulwark**	moreover	barrier	synchronicity	oxymoron	labyrinth

B. Fill in the blanks

Fill in the blanks from the words in the table below. There are two extra words you do not need.

buoyant	topically	absolute	anesthetic	beguile	denigrate	libertarian

1. The doctor said the ointment needed to be applied _____.

2. The treatment will be done under _____.

3. The trickster was clever enough to _____ everyone around.

4. The camera was lost in the ocean since it wasn't _____.

5. The rules are _____ and there aren't any exceptions.

C. Homophones and homographs

Homophones are two or more words having the same pronunciation but different spellings and meanings. Homographs are words which have the same spelling but different meanings.

From the list below, fill in the blanks.

oh	addition	moped	edition	owe	wind

1. A vehicle with two wheels   _____

2. An expression   _____

3. To turn round and round   _____

4. To be in debt   _____

5. Movement of air   _____

6. Felt dejected and sulked   _____

7. Add extra   _____

8. A version of a text   _____

D. Synonyms - Spelling

Complete the synonym of the word in **bold**.

1. **crafty**   d __ __ __ o u s

2. **bibulous**   d __ u n k __ __

3. **malapropism**   m __ __ u s e

4. **recondite**   o __ s c u r __

5. **bruit**   r __ __ o r

6. **braggadocious**   b __ __ __ t f u l

7. **discombobulated**   c o n __ u __ e d

Set 20

A. Synonyms

Select the word that most closely matches the meaning of the word provided.

1.	**humane**	omniscient	flamboyant	benevolent	potent	panicked
2.	**illustrious**	shallow	implicit	joyful	eminent	obtrude
3.	**whimsical**	dignified	magnified	confidential	simple	capricious
4.	**utmost**	maximum	standard	moderate	irrupted	cordial
5.	**torpid**	rigorous	sever	slow	staged	exacting
6.	**sunder**	whack	upheave	innovate	revive	divide
7.	**somnolence**	confer	effective	stupor	dynamic	free
8.	**ruminate**	holler	cogitate	loosen	merge	brusque

B. Missing words

Choose the best word to complete the sentences.

The local library is more than just a place for books. There is a (1)_____(throng, thrive, thresh) of other resources. (2)_____(rejuvenate, wander, meddle) around the shelves and you'll find DVDs and audiobooks among the more traditional paper books. If history is your thing, why not (3)_____(inquire, question, news) about books, newspaper clippings, and special events happening in your community? Libraries often (4)_____(disrupt, asks, invite) guest speakers to give talks! Everyone is welcome. Check out your local library and you might just be (5)_____(astounded, frustrated, likened) at what they have on offer.

C. Antonyms

Pick the word that means the opposite or near opposite of the word provided.

1.	**influx**	citadel	chateau	preposterous	hideous	outflow
2.	**pallor**	flush	crush	destruct	pester	deliberate
3.	**embroil**	infringe	extricate	absolve	uphold	examine
4.	**abase**	determine	embark	falsify	extol	socialize
5.	**abet**	confound	dissuade	campaign	prize	track
6.	**barter**	exculpate	hint	keep	revise	affix
7.	**abdicate**	stage	dispute	dethrone	conquer	accept
8.	**abstemious**	intemperate	inform	braid	plaid	incurable

D. Idioms

Match each idiom to its meaning.

1. **A dime a dozen**   a. All the time

2. **Accident waiting to happen**   b. Inexpensive

3. **Around the clock**   c. Someone you love

4. **Bad egg**   d. Missed opportunity

5. **Apple of my eye**   e. Dangerous, hazardous

6. **On solid ground**   f. Immoral, not a good person

7. **Miss the boat**   g. Safe and secure

Set 21

A. Synonyms

Select the word that most closely matches the meaning of the word provided.

1. **reconcile**   untie   disengage   upscale   renovate   reunite

2. **prudent**   rash   charred   judicious   premiere   brutal

3. **maxim**   headboard   contraband   motto   dictionary   sleeve

4. **ostentatious** godly   laughable   pretentious desperate   musky

5. **heretic**   unbeliever   deceiver   receiver   cleaver   believer

6. **gainsay**   challenge   meeting   seminar   lesson   observation

7. **facetious**   sacred   solemn   elegant   spectating   jocular

8. **epithet**   setting   trio   hashtag   moniker   mild

B. Fill in the blanks

Fill in the blanks from the words in the table below. There are two extra words you do not need.

articulate	euphemism	aristocratic	dwelling	bibliophile	intractable	ingenious

1. The student was a _____, that's why she enjoyed visiting the library so much.

2. The Kraken is a mythical sea _____ creature.

3. Some topics were hard to discuss; many _____s were used.

4. Some of the silliest of inventions are actually _____.

5. When I can't _____ my thoughts, I take a deep breath and try again.

C. Homophones and homographs

Homophones are two or more words having the same pronunciation but different spellings and meanings. Homographs are words which have the same spelling but different meanings.

From the list below, fill in the blanks.

to	brake	break	console	too	crane

1.   Resting time   _____

2.   In addition   _____

3.   A set of controls or instruments   _____

4.   A preposition   _____

5.   Device for slowing a vehicle   _____

6.   A bird   _____

7.   Make someone feel better   _____

8.   A piece of equipment used for lifting heavy objects   _____

D. Synonyms - Spelling

Complete the synonym of the word in **bold**.

1. **perish**   d __ __

2. **quench**   d __ __ s __

3. **alienate**   i s __ l __ __ e

4. **business**   f __ r m

5. **authenticate**   v __ __ i f __

6. **scholarly**   __ c a __ e m __ c

7. **debatable**   d __ __ p u t __ b l e

Set 22

A. Synonyms

Select the word that most closely matches the meaning of the word provided.

1.	**egalitarian**	charismatic	democratic	static	piratic	skeptic
2.	**dauntless**	fearless	expressive	truth	kindness	impress
3.	**conflagration**	fireplace	machinery	oven	silverware	inferno
4.	**wheedle**	maggoty	associate	coax	rivet	please
5.	**usurp**	postulate	arrogate	give away	dramatize	sit-down
6.	**bashfully**	finally	ultimately	ruthlessly	terminally	sheepishly
7.	**recognizance**	bond	chain	bind	glue	lace
8.	**perpetuity**	joy	eternity	humility	cowardice	harmonious

B. Missing words

Choose the best word to complete the sentences.

How many hours do you use your cell phone? Research has (1)_____(seen, suggest, shown)

that on average, people use their phones for around 3 hours every day. While cell phones can be

(2)_____(handy, nuisance, switched), their (3)_____(predictive,

vindictive, addictive) nature can be damaging. Staring at a phone screen for so long can cause

(4)_____(loose, excruciating, crumbling) headaches and sore eyes. That's why it's

best to (5)_____(watching, monitor, administer) screen time.

C. Antonyms

Pick the word that means the opposite or near opposite of the word provided.

1.	**squander**	deprave	portray	throw	save	lay
2.	**staccato**	legato	enslave	finite	crude	consume
3.	**appreciable**	niche	taught	negligible	moldable	rumpled
4.	**autocratic**	automatic	pensive	defensive	applauded	democratic
5.	**blanch**	color	scrape	chop	grate	cream
6.	**blasphemy**	reverence	sweltering	thickness	meditating	assembly
7.	**concerted**	assembled	triage	assistance	individual	colleague
8.	**contend**	remember	surrender	reimburse	adverse	prize

D. Idioms

Match each idiom to its meaning.

1.	**A stone's throw away**	a. Refuse to confront or solve
2.	**All ears**	b. Ordinary
3.	**Couch potato**	c. Have second thoughts
4.	**Bog standard**	d. Lazy person
5.	**Bury your head in the sand**	e. Very nearby
6.	**Call a spade a spade**	f. Listening carefully
7.	**Cold feet**	g. Speak frankly and directly

Set 23

A. Synonyms

Select the word that most closely matches the meaning of the word provided.

1.	**nefarious**	iniquitous	virtuous	intriguing	stark	dreary
2.	**maudlin**	sarcastic	sentimental	spiteful	momentous	domestic
3.	**lenient**	bothersome	intrusive	inquisitive	tolerant	strengthened
4.	**intrinsic**	temperate	brash	courageous	luxurious	inherent
5.	**heinous**	atrocious	sweet	esteemed	massive	radical
6.	**fusillade**	salvo	washed	tinkled	park	trench
7.	**effrontery**	audacity	elasticity	plasticity	capacity	electricity
8.	**cynical**	paranoid	known	branched	distrustful	compliant

B. Fill in the blanks

Fill in the blanks from the words in the table below. There are two extra words you do not need.

attitude	toothsome	pontificate	critter	eloquent	isthmus	ingénue

1. The pope passed away after a _____ of ten years.

2. The _____ in the bug house was fascinating to watch.

3. He was _____ in the way he spoke.

4. A bad _____ will land you in detention.

5. The actress changed from her usual rowdy roles, to playing an _____ role.

C. Homophones and homographs

Homophones are two or more words having the same pronunciation but different spellings and meanings. Homographs are words which have the same spelling but different meanings.

From the list below, fill in the blanks.

drape	complement	capital	lead	capitol	compliment

1.   A curtain   _____

2.   The main city   _____

3.   A kind remark   _____

4.   The way in which a garment hangs   _____

5.   A type of metal   _____

6.   Something that completes another thing nicely   _____

7.   Where Congress meets   _____

8.   To take charge   _____

D. Synonyms - Spelling

Complete the synonym of the word in **bold**.

1. **consummate**   p __ __ f __ c t

2. **absentee**   t r __ __ n t

3. **convalescence**   r __ __ o v __ r y

4. **decree**   __ __ w

5. **consternation**   __ __ s m a y

6. **gist**   e __ s e n __ __

7. **permeated**   i __ __ u s e d

Set 24

A. Synonyms

Select the word that most closely matches the meaning of the word provided.

1.	**ambrosial**	cordial	heavenly	warren	burrow	scampi
2.	**acrid**	fueled	frightened	crucible	pungent	whiny
3.	**brutal**	cruel	scrawny	foremost	esteemed	dazed
4.	**sojourn**	pullover	sleepover	moreover	stopover	win over
5.	**abrogate**	punch	annul	birth	disguise	invest
6.	**suffuse**	shepherd	translate	advance	atomize	tinge
7.	**rudimentary**	complex	primitive	advanced	agonizing	frumpy
8.	**timorous**	parched	serene	afraid	bored	proud

B. Missing words

Choose the best word to complete the sentences.

The power of pets is truly (1)_____(magnified, magnificent, magnitude). There has

been extensive (2)_____(research, reclaim, retest) regarding pets and their link to our

health. The (3)_____(lookings, searchings, findings) have shown that having a pet can

lower the amount of cortisol (a hormone related to stress) in the body and even lower blood

(4)_____(pressing, pressure, levels). So, unless you have an

(5)_____(cat, allergy, sibling), the only question left is: which pet are you going to get?

C. Antonyms

Pick the word that means the opposite or near opposite of the word provided.

1.	**cerebral**	absolved	pragmatic	unlettered	written	boisterous
2.	**parlay**	procreated	unforgiving	dwindle	nervy	pragmatic
3.	**fluster**	calm	raucous	hunch	muscular	gassy
4.	**regnant**	impotent	staunch	laborious	delightful	baggy
5.	**fabricated**	startled	detailed	frenetic	unknown	legitimate
6.	**ignoble**	calamitous	noble	corpulent	jejune	friable
7.	**clerisy**	commoner	coroner	moniker	borrower	controller
8.	**wail**	wiggle	giggle	sniggle	tickle	niggle

D. Idioms

Match each idiom to its meaning.

1.	**Cut a long story short**	a. Competitive
2.	**Dig one's heels in**	b. Extremely hungry
3.	**Dog eat dog**	c. Don't try to do something difficult without learning the basics
4.	**Don't put all your eggs in one basket**	d. An important topic nobody wants to discuss
5.	**I could eat a horse**	e. Be diverse in your efforts
6.	**Don't run before you can walk**	f. Explain in few words
7.	**Elephant in the room**	g. Stay true to your opinion or argument

Set 25

A. Synonyms

Select the word that most closely matches the meaning of the word provided.

1.	**peripheral**	substance	reef	outer	wise	rot
2.	**ossify**	harden	trudge	plunge	compose	reprove
3.	**nebulous**	hazy	invidious	snobby	obnoxious	execrable
4.	**maelstrom**	memoir	chronicle	pier	debutant	vortex
5.	**leery**	coddle	dangly	suspicious	particular	spirally
6.	**intrigue**	scheme	potion	spork	nosey	pedantic
7.	**indomitable**	wordless	courageous	nimble	horrendous	effusive
8.	**hegemony**	troop	squad	trainees	authority	pupils

B. Fill in the blanks

Fill in the blanks from the words in the table below. There are two extra words you do not need.

depleted	interlope	miserly	tankard	nepotism	mutiny	docile

1. The resources became _____ so the group had to think about rationing in the future.

2. Violent acts of _____ have dire consequences.

3. The company owners wanted _____ workers who wouldn't argue or vent their frustration.

4. Her _____ behavior was embarrassing to be around, especially when it came to tipping in restaurants.

5. The worker must have got the job through _____ because he was extremely unskilled.

C. Homophones and homographs

Homophones are two or more words having the same pronunciation but different spellings and meanings. Homographs are words which have the same spelling but different meanings.

From the list below, fill in the blanks.

sewer	wound	banned	mare	mayor	band

1. Prohibited   _____

2. A high ranking official   _____

3. A female horse   _____

4. A musical group   _____

5. Someone who sews   _____

6. An injury   _____

7. Underground network for waste   _____

8. Past tense of wind   _____

D. Synonyms - Spelling

Complete the synonym of the word in **bold**.

1. **mores**   c __ __ t o m

2. **lecture**   s __ e e __ __

3. **partisan**   b __ __ s e d

4. **per capita**   p __ __ p e r __ o n

5. **supine**   p a __ __ i v e

6. **tedium**   m __ __ o t __ n y

7. **probation**   p __ __ o l e

Set 26

A. Synonyms

Select the word that most closely matches the meaning of the word provided.

1.	**caricature**	calamity	mishap	parody	charcoal	gauche
2.	**brink**	incognito	disguise	ruler	middle	edge
3.	**wane**	wax	peat	sundry	macho	decline
4.	**sobriety**	arrogance	abstinence	disagreement	greed	willingness
5.	**ruddy**	rosy	azure	hew	tingle	yellowed
6.	**recalcitrant**	easygoing	defiant	inhumane	insane	reliant
7.	**quixotic**	idealistic	improvised	second wave	focused	spiced
8.	**proviso**	fruition	audition	expenditure	condition	rendition

B. Missing words

Choose the best word to complete the sentences.

When you think about skincare, what usually springs to mind? Luxurious face masks, vitamins, fruit scents? These are all common, but did you know that some skincare contains snail mucin? Mucin is the slimy (1)_____(things, item, substance) we are all too familiar with. Mucin contains a number of skin-(2)_____(making, dwelling, loving) ingredients. After using, the skin is said to be (3)_____(grimier, plumper, softness) than ever. Although it might sound (4)_____(horror, grotesque, gripe), snail mucin has become a skincare (5)_____(link, strap, staple) for dozens of men and women.

C. Antonyms

Pick the word that means the opposite or near opposite of the word provided.

1.	**senile**	depressed	melancholy	destitute	sharp	devastating
2.	**apathetic**	passionate	incendiary	hot	infallible	deceptive
3.	**pristine**	serene	implied	wholesome	outdoorsy	dirty
4.	**catastrophic**	puckish	fortunate	implied	posted	frostbite
5.	**stoical**	minatory	emotional	ill humored	rebarbative	saturated
6.	**paradox**	enigma	explanation	puzzle	loiter	mystery
7.	**platonic**	playful	flamboyant	iridescent	romantic	designed
8.	**savor**	shun	sham	shot	shale	shingles

D. Idioms

Match each idiom to its meaning.

1.	**Don't give up your day job**	a. Face the unpleasant consequences of your actions
2.	**Face the music**	b. Become comfortable, knowledgeable
3.	**Eat your words**	c. Become vexed
4.	**Finger in every pie**	d. Admit you are wrong
5.	**Get off my back**	e. The expression used in jest to tell a person they are not good at something
6.	**Freak out**	f. Be involved in a large and varied number of activities
7.	**Find your feet**	g. Stop berating me

Set 27

A. Synonyms

Select the word that most closely matches the meaning of the word provided.

1. **peripatetic**   settled   fixed   itinerant   gluttonous   spiteful

2. **indolent**   idle   clandestine   diligent   sagacious   luminous

3. **exuberant**   friable   insolent   ebullient   emollient   soothing

4. **epiphany**   termination   aberration   rendition   revelation   abjuration

5. **diaphanous**   opaque   grisly   grimy   slimy   transparent

6. **cursory**   theoretical   wonderful   hasty   whimsical   theatrical

7. **mar**   spoil   spell   intertwine   reconcile   categorize

8. **lavish**   limpid   bony   spiny   opulent   charismatic

B. Fill in the blanks

Fill in the blanks from the words in the table below. There are two extra words you do not need.

temerity	dexterity	strenuous	trounce	apprised	lander	tenuous

1. The builders had a great deal of _____ work ahead of them.

2. They know an expert who can _____ anyone in a game.

3. It took some _____, but the boy finally asked his crush on a date.

4. They _____ the students a week before the project was due.

5. The ice was broken with a _____ chortle.

C. Homophones and homographs

Homophones are two or more words having the same pronunciation but different spellings and meanings. Homographs are words which have the same spelling but different meanings.

From the list below, fill in the blanks.

steak	stalk	back	accent	stake	stork

1. A body part   _____

2. A tall bird   _____

3. Part of a flower or plant   _____

4. A piece of meat   _____

5. The way words are pronounced   _____

6. Emphasize   _____

7. Opposite of front   _____

8. A wooden or metal pole with a point   _____

D. Synonyms - Spelling

Complete the synonym of the word in **bold**.

1. **truculent**   f __ e r __ e

2. **trivial**   p __ __ t y

3. **besmirch**   s u __ __ y

4. **cogent**   v __ l i __

5. **fervent**   a __ __ e n t

6. **succulent**   j u i __ __

7. **cerebral**   m e n __ __ l

Set 28

A. Synonyms

Select the word that most closely matches the meaning of the word provided.

1.	**laconic**	finite	brief	paradoxical	iconic	tampered
2.	**capitulate**	tempered	summit	crucial	submit	curt
3.	**undulate**	cell	jell	folly	toll	roll
4.	**condescend**	patronize	care for	carbonize	multisite	paralyze
5.	**manumit**	set free	give up	carefree	turn up	fill out
6.	**orator**	doctor	lecturer	anesthetist	mechanic	engineer
7.	**nadir**	high	level	flat	low	intermediate
8.	**potentate**	monarch	disciple	peasant	drone	adherent

B. Missing words

Choose the best word to complete the sentences.

Who would have thought that (1) _____ (residing, live, meandering) in our very eyelashes are (2) _____(minute, hour, coping) mites? They are so tiny that they cannot be seen unless under a (3) _____ (microscope, telescope, horoscope). Do not be (4) _____ (petulant, pride, perturbed) by the little critters, though! Most people do not suffer from them in the (5) _____ (lightest, slightest, highest).

C. Antonyms

Pick the word that means the opposite or near opposite of the word provided.

1.	**vicissltudes**	uniformity	abnormality	theatrically	fluctuation	joyfully
2.	**swarthy**	kinetic	enwalled	light	envisaged	marry
3.	**sartorial**	polyamorous	quaver	mere	tailored	unstylish
4.	**pendulous**	retreat	raised	retire	drooping	cobalt
5.	**zealot**	fortify	haggard	unbiased	extortion	fodder
6.	**stingy**	neutral	naive	urgent	scarce	generous
7.	**specious**	abstemious	sundial	levitate	afflicted	valid
8.	**parsimonious**	quadrant	parsley	pasture	companion	altruistic

D. Idioms

Match each idiom to its meaning.

1. **Fit as a fiddle**   a. To be highly, uncannily observant

2. **Get one's act together**   b. Give up an addiction abruptly

3. **Glad to see the back of someone**   c. Very fit, healthy

4. **Go cold turkey**   d. Be in a bad mood

5. **Get up on the wrong side of the bed**   e. Organize one's affairs

6. **Eyes in the back of one's head**   f. Do the same as someone else did before

7. **Follow in someone's footsteps**   g. Be happy that a relationship ended

Set 29

A. Synonyms

Select the word that most closely matches the meaning of the word provided.

1.	**frugal**	astrology	caffeinated	oneness	harried	economical
2.	**impecunious**	wealthy	pest	laughable	extended	penniless
3.	**indistinct**	decomposed	destitute	hazy	abstained	dyed
4.	**ephemeral**	fleeting	multitude	multilingual	hoarse	chauvinistic
5.	**desirous**	placid	covetous	misogynistic	coarse	troubled
6.	**concur**	cogent	agree	correlated	stalk	made up
7.	**bellicose**	pacifist	wondrous	triage	truculent	foliage
8.	**amass**	scouring	jeer	hoard	biopic	disperse

B. Fill in the blanks

Fill in the blanks from the words in the table below. There are two extra words you do not need.

fallible	congeal	tripe	chimerical	bogus	fathom	foible

1. The _____ caller turned out to be my sister playing a practical joke.

2. To think all rules will be abided by is _____.

3. They watched the solution _____ into a jelly-like substance.

4. Even the smartest of us are _____.

5. Nobody could _____ out the reason for the boy's intransigence.

C. Homophones and homographs

Homophones are two or more words having the same pronunciation but different spellings and meanings. Homographs are words which have the same spelling but different meanings.

From the list below, fill in the blanks.

genes	cock	watt	jeans	chest	what

1.   A trunk   _____

2.   Denim trousers   _____

3.   Unit of electric power   _____

4.   Hereditary units   _____

5.   Part of the body   _____

6.   Get a gun ready to fire   _____

7.   A question word   _____

8.   Tilting motion   _____

D. Synonyms - Spelling

Complete the synonym of the word in **bold**.

1. **avarice**   c u p __ __ __ t y

2. **clobber**   h i __

3. **grumble**   c __ __ p __ a i __

4. **philanthropic** h __ __ a n i t a r i a n

5. **lawn**   g __ __ d __ __

6. **bounty**   r e __ a r __

7. **polyglot**   m u __ __ __ l i n g u a l

Set 30

A. Synonyms

Select the word that most closely matches the meaning of the word provided.

1.	**cupidity**	avarice	sourness	boastful	difficult	bibliophile
2.	**capacious**	turbulent	exact	roomy	studious	diligent
3.	**unobtrusive**	abundant	discreet	coherent	obtaining	leeching
4.	**riveting**	fortuitous	nihilism	abysmal	dire	gripping
5.	**prosperous**	coniferous	haughty	cheeky	affluent	wicked
9.	**perforate**	pierce	treacherous	hindrance	helpful	abstentious
10.	**concise**	feline	compact	enormous	freed	exonerate
11.	**cantankerous**	overjoyed	motto	cranky	reconciled	epithet

B. Missing words

Choose the best word to complete the sentences.

Have you ever heard of a funambulist? It's a fancy word which in (1)_____(layman's, seamen's, fancy) terms means a tightrope walker. The term (2)_____(petals, thorns, stems) from the latin 'funis' meaning 'rope' and 'ambulare' meaning 'walk'. Becoming a funambulist is not an easy (3)_____(toe, feet, feat). One must have concentration, determination, and a range of other (4)_____(gratitude, attributes, latitudes) to do well and (5)_____(prosper, preposterous, perspire). Have you got what it takes to become a funambulist?

C. Antonyms

Pick the word that means the opposite or near opposite of the word provided.

1.	**conceal**	announce	denounce	pronounce	council	melodious
2.	**tractable**	consecrated	deafening	defiant	brass	flashed
3.	**spurn**	dissolved	odious	fanciful	turnstile	accept
4.	**salubrious**	gentlemanly	killjoy	jamming	harmful	studious
5.	**hurry**	unite	berate	dawdle	spamming	tribute
6.	**induct**	install	reject	drone	scan	handover
7.	**heckle**	support	bash	haggle	barter	acidify
8.	**ally**	enemy	repugnant	superfood	probe	substantiation

D. Idioms

Match each idiom to its meaning.

1. **Head over heels**   a. Wait

2. **Ignorance is bliss**   b. Stay positive

3. **Hold your horses**   c. Not knowing doesn't hurt

4. **Keep your chin up**   d. Try every possible course of action

5. **Jump ship**   e. Not difficult

6. **It's not rocket science** f. In deep love

7. **Leave no stone unturned** g. Leave an organization or cause

Set 31

A. Synonyms

Select the word that most closely matches the meaning of the word provided.

1.	**accrue**	gather	felicity	decrease	artifice	obscure
2.	**hypothetical**	dormant	latent	futile	theoretical	artifact
3.	**opprobrium**	candor	spew	shame	lame	calamity
4.	**perfidious**	negligible	hereditary	ladylike	beatified	treacherous
5.	**portend**	party	rejoice	augur	command	fantasize
6.	**preeminent**	dormant	leading	murky	querulous	grouchy
7.	**ravenous**	libertarian	egalitarian	bookish	greedy	balding
8.	**proscribe**	advertise	alter	prohibit	predispose	trivial

B. Fill in the blanks

Fill in the blanks from the words in the table below. There are two extra words you do not need.

egregious	verdant	wheedling	tenacious	sagacious	linchpin	levy

1. She was the _____ of the Olympic team.

2. The _____ forests of the country were a national treasure.

3. It took him months of _____ and cajoling to finally get what he wanted.

4. The _____ lawyer was hired all over the city.

5. The mishap was so _____that I start trembling when I think about it.

C. Homophones and homographs

Homophones are two or more words having the same pronunciation but different spellings and meanings. Homographs are words which have the same spelling but different meanings.

From the list below, fill in the blanks.

pie	content	peddle	pedal	pi	fall

1.   The place your foot goes on a bike   _____

2.   A baked treat   _____

3.   Lose balance   _____

4.   Part of mathematics and the Greek alphabet   _____

5.   Happy   _____

6.   Try to sell something   _____

7.   One of the seasons   _____

8.   Things that are kept somewhere or held in something   _____

D. Synonyms - Spelling

Complete the synonym of the word in **bold**.

1. **philosophical**   t __ __ u g h t f __ l

2. **parenthesis**   b __ __ __ c k e t s

3. **sacrilege**   v __ __ __ l a t i o __

4. **plead**   b __ __ __

5. **lucid**   c l __ __ __ r

6. **vanguard**   f o __ __ __ f r __ __ __ t

7. **annoyance**   v __ __ __ a t i o n

Set 32

A. Synonyms

Select the word that most closely matches the meaning of the word provided.

1.	**enthrall**	banish	captivate	obvious	accent	revel
2.	**indigent**	blanch	stalky	opulent	savage	needy
3.	**lassitude**	exhaustion	precipitate	accelerate	lavish	arrow
4.	**malodorous**	rosy	appealing	fetid	teasing	gratuitous
5.	**conciliate**	fugitive	interim	mollify	graft	succumb
6.	**calumny**	slander	softly	incorporate	acclaim	burrows
7.	**defy**	commune	yearn	stern	oppose	extreme
8.	**servant**	stun	solidify	lecture	drudge	blotch

B. Missing words

Choose the best word to complete the sentences.

Being eco-warriors these days involves much more than cutting your shower short and driving less. From bamboo toothbrushes and toilet paper, to reusable sanitary products and more, there are dozens of ways to help the planet. One (1)_____(temporarily, reasoned, arguably) extreme way of (2)_____(improving, degrading, masking) the health of our planet is by giving up meat and fish. Scientists and environmentalists have shown that by (3)_____(abstaining, draining, elongating) from eating meat and fish, the impact one has on the environment is decreased. (4)_____(Congress, Digress, Nevertheless), there are other factors that contribute to the poor health of the world. Which leaves the question: Where do we (5)_____(sketch, paint, draw) the line?

C. Antonyms

Pick the word that means the opposite or near opposite of the word provided.

1.	**enrage**	direct	tractable	miser	vane	placate
2.	**quaint**	usual	scenic	hexagonal	existential	equine
3.	**subtle**	peaceful	submissive	summit	obvious	charged up
4.	**indifferent**	eloquence	separation	industrial	network	fervent
5.	**compulsion**	suppress	apprehend	choice	amend	emulate
6.	**cleave**	scratch	graze	blow	loop	join
7.	**collective**	commit	reconcile	join forces	party	individual
8.	**animosity**	marriage	love	distressed	narcissism	fascism

D. Idioms

Match each idiom to its meaning.

1. **Let sleeping dogs lie**   a. Cause disruption

2. **Look a million dollars**   b. Spend a lot of money on something

3. **Pull someone's leg**   c. Trick someone in a playful way

4. **Rock the boat**   d. Don't disturb a situation that is currently causing no issues

5. **Splash out**   e. To be suspicious

6. **No-brainer**   f. Look extremely extravagant, beautiful

7. **Smell a rat**   g. Something obvious, needing no mental effort

Set 33

A. Synonyms

Select the word that most closely matches the meaning of the word provided.

1.	**surmise**	ironclad	mechanic	purposeful	suppose	irate
2.	**mutiny**	rivaling	unobtrusive	rebellion	appealing	affluent
3.	**haughty**	appalling	perforated	carbonated	proud	furious
4.	**impassioned**	prosperous	frugal	cursive	intense	fathomable
5.	**frank**	flatulent	diaphanous	sumptuous	candid	extrapolates
6.	**malleable**	swanky	deciding	embedding	ductile	reminding
7.	**largesse**	munificence	heredity	torrid	polity	magnitude
8.	**enrapture**	bore	fascinate	fob off	shoulder	abominate

B. Fill in the blanks

Fill in the blanks from the words in the table below. There are two extra words you do not need.

figurative	haughty	internecine	goosebumps	kindle	fleeting	iconoclastic

1. His views were revolutionary and _____.

2. The eerie tale gave every member of the reading group _____.

3. _____ language is used throughout the author's works.

4. Their relationship had become _____, so they decided to call it a day.

5. The fans caught a _____ look of their beloved singer.

C. Homophones and homographs

Homophones are two or more words having the same pronunciation but different spellings and meanings. Homographs are words which have the same spelling but different meanings.

From the list below, fill in the blanks.

hoard	horde	kernel	colonel	well	wave

1.   Good, healthy   _____

2.   A hand gesture   _____

3.   A large unorganized group of individuals   _____

4.   A seed in a shell   _____

5.   A depression made to hold liquids   _____

6.   A store or stock of valued objects   _____

7.   Sea water curling into an arch   _____

8.   A ranking officer   _____

D. Synonyms - Spelling

Complete the synonym of the word in **bold**.

1. **adieu**   f __ r __ __ e l l

2. **roost**   p __ __ c h

3. **diffident**   __ __ s i t a n t

4. **grotesque**   i n __ __ n g r u o u s

5. **groggy**   d __ z __ d

6. **erratic**   i r r e __ __ l a r

7. **flinders**   s p l __ __ t e r s

Set 34

A. Synonyms

Select the word that most closely matches the meaning of the word provided.

1.	**servile**	evince	tactile	knocking	block	obsequious
2.	**rhetorical**	holistic	sweetly	likened	bombastic	linked
3.	**rectitude**	limberness	willingness	broken	stationery	integrity
4.	**uncouth**	gorgeous	heavenly	manifesto	coarse	beautiful
5.	**muster**	destroy	covet	parchment	scrolled	gather
12.	**onerous**	sloth like	thirty	edible	revenue	arduous
13.	**penurious**	give up	hard up	look up	put up	put off
14.	**harp**	goblet	trunk	repeat	squash	champion

B. Missing words

Choose the best word to complete the sentences.

Diwali is a festival of great importance in Hinduism. The festival (1)_____(translates, linguist, reimagines) as a festival of lights and (2)_____(presets, ignites, represents) light overcoming darkness and knowledge overcoming obliviousness. During the festival period, people wear their (3)_____(golden, finest, silver lined) clothes, exchange gifts, set off (4)_____(candles, fireworks, greetings), spend time with loved ones, and of course, pray. The festival period usually lasts for five days, but lasts for six in some (5)_____(countries, continents, regions) of India.

C. Antonyms

Pick the word that means the opposite or near opposite of the word provided.

1.	**dexterous**	leprosy	maladroit	plating	expert	prohibit
2.	**draconian**	subnormal	leotard	tubular	percussion	mild
3.	**microscopic**	gosling	governance	colossal	replete	tiny
4.	**jejune**	quotidian	interesting	rabid	kneader	plasma
5.	**romanticize**	degrade	legislative	raconteur	idealize	exalt
6.	**savage**	subject	suborn	relocate	kind	ectoplasm
7.	**long-winded**	egocentric	short	clammy	gratuitous	coniferous
8.	**staffed**	squeaky	classical	unmanned	clapper	clavicle

D. Idioms

Match each idiom to its meaning.

1.	**Jump on the bandwagon**	a. Don't believe every word
2.	**Bigger fish to fry**	b. The most beautiful woman at the party
3.	**Turn the tables**	c. Change the situation so now you have the advantage
4.	**Take it with a pinch of salt**	d. Eat
5.	**Belle of the ball**	e. Follow a trend
6.	**Chow down**	f. Private information that should not be asked about
7.	**None of your business**	g. To have more important issues to attend to

Set 35

A. Synonyms

Select the word that most closely matches the meaning of the word provided.

1.	**eclectic**	commission	foreseeable	varied	minister	provoke
2.	**serendipity**	overwhelm	luck	negotiation	terrorist	dissolution
3.	**munificent**	authentic	mandate	broker	charitable	aspire
4.	**camaraderie**	experiment	bacterial	intermittent	nested	fellowship
5.	**baneful**	pernicious	nationalize	salubrious	preserve	anodyne
6.	**pessimistic**	cynical	prehistoric	optimistic	fraction	philately
7.	**blissful**	population	predestined	ecstatic	melancholy	ceremonious
8.	**fluctuate**	alternate	rock	phenol	extensive	solemnize

B. Fill in the blanks

Fill in the blanks from the words in the table below. There are two extra words you do not need.

reason	fortuitous	occur	reason	axis	seasons	tremendously

1. The earth's _____ is an imaginary pole going through the center of the earth from the top to the

2. bottom. The earth rotates around its axis. This is the _____

3. why day and night _____. Also, the earth's axis is tilted!

4. Which is why we have four _____. The reason for the axis not being straight

5. is believed to be a collision with a _____ large object a long time ago.

C. Homophones and homographs

Homophones are two or more words having the same pronunciation but different spellings and meanings. Homographs are words which have the same spelling but different meanings.

From the list below, fill in the blanks.

hanger	float	crews	fast	hangar	cruise

1. Used to hang clothing   _____

2. A holiday on a ship   _____

3. Refrain from eating   _____

4. Antonym of drown   _____

5. Synonym of teams   _____

6. Where aircrafts are kept   _____

7. Quick   _____

8. Drift slowly and lightly in air   _____

D. Synonyms - Spelling

Complete the synonym of the word in **bold**.

1. **disregard**   t __ __ o w   a w a y

2. **consecrate**   s __ __ c t i f y

3. **shallow**   s __ __ e r __ i c i a l

4. **empire**   __ __ m a i n

5. **dimension**   m __ __ s u r e m e n t

6. **territory**   __ __ __ v __ n c e

7. **abundant**   c __ p i o __ s

Set 36

A. Synonyms

Select the word that most closely matches the meaning of the word provided.

1.	**coerce**	pressurize	persuade	emanate	transmit	produce
2.	**flabbergasted**	stupefied	deposit	swollen	admin	historian
3.	**construe**	optical	gladiolus	take	exceeds	paramilitary
4.	**connive**	scheme	varied	eclectic	supervise	densify
5.	**keen**	conform	administer	eager	haughty	pernicious
6.	**insatiable**	allied	janky	compromised	voracious	occupied
7.	**erudite**	aviator	impolite	methane	fatigued	scholarly
8.	**hypocrite**	genuine	frank	phony	honest	creed

B. Missing words

Choose the best word to complete the sentences.

Chess is a game with plenty of (1)_____(grooves, moves, tunes), making it one of the hardest games to master. There are six (2)_____(kinds, minds, rooks) of chess pieces, the most powerful being the queen. The queen is able to move vertically, horizontally, and (3)_____(immortally, skeletally, diagonally). The queen is also not limited to moving only one square. The king, (4)_____(on the side, on the other leg, on the other hand), does not hold such (5)_____(piece, grace, power).

C. Antonyms

Pick the word that means the opposite or near opposite of the word provided.

1.	**hypothetical**	mirage	unlawful	actual	remark	offset
2.	**abeyant**	solder	active	mound	puppet	farcical
3.	**insolence**	quoted	bloated	ambitious	modesty	ornate
4.	**discernment**	idiocy	unyielding	colloquial	canine	incredible
5.	**ebullience**	adamant	crapulous	depression	effulgent	sagacious
6.	**indefatigable**	zealous	jealous	hardworking	managerial	work-shy
7.	**inconsistent**	clerical	concise	spherical	consistent	precise
8.	**zenith**	base	peak	weak	meek	leak

D. Idioms

Match each idiom to its meaning.

1. **Drive someone nuts**   a. Instantly

2. **Have it up to here**   b. Too late and insignificant

3. **You know the drill**   c. To be familiar with

4. **In a New York minute**   d. An estimate

5. **A ballpark figure**   e. To stop something

6. **Put the brakes on**   f. Annoy someone

7. **A day late and a dollar short**   g. Be tired of the situation

Set 37

A. Synonyms

Select the word that most closely matches the meaning of the word provided.

1.	**dubious**	uncertain	detonated	restful	zestful	woozy
2.	**exactitude**	precision	chaotic	muddled	compatible	jugular
3.	**abridge**	abbreviate	look up	enchant	string	ting
4.	**ubiquitous**	individualistic	honed	impaired	corrugated	universal
5.	**equanimity**	composure	exposure	closure	lackluster	flustered
6.	**unflappable**	answerable	placid	dilated	excitable	dynamic
7.	**jittery**	mocked	jumpy	ordinary	paramount	fleecy
8.	**idiosyncratic**	boring	garrulous	quirky	slipshod	exquisite

B. Fill in the blanks

Fill in the blanks from the words in the table below. There are two extra words you do not need.

biodiversity	obliterated	logging	gargantuan	coverage	necessary	diseases

1. The Amazon Rainforest is a _____ rainforest located in South America.

2. Famous for its _____, many believe that the cure for

3. various _____ can be found there.

4. Unfortunately however, the Amazon is being _____ at an alarming rate.

5. The introductory course did not offer sufficient _____ of the subject.

C. Homophones and homographs

Homophones are two or more words having the same pronunciation but different spellings and meanings. Homographs are words which have the same spelling but different meanings.

From the list below, fill in the blanks.

scent	match	we'd	sent	implant	weed

1. Past tense of send   _____

2. A contraction of we had   _____

3. Insert something by surgery   _____

4. Pleasant smell   _____

5. A wooden stick used to ignite   _____

6. An unwanted plant   _____

7. Identical to another person or thing   _____

8. A prosthetic body part   _____

D. Synonyms - Spelling

Complete the synonym of the word in **bold**.

1. **grove**   o__ __ h a r d

2. **gesticulate** s __ __ n a l

3. **bend**   __ __ o o p

4. **hit**   w h __ c __

5. **mobster**   g __ __ g s t e __

6. **taboo**   __ o r b i d __ __ __

7. **ecstatic**   e __ __ h o r i __

Set 38

A. Synonyms

Select the word that most closely matches the meaning of the word provided.

1.	**extraneous**	arrogant	irrelevant	petulant	persistent	coexist
2.	**quiescent**	excitable	bubbling	inactive	broiling	jostling
3.	**prodigal**	savior	extrapolate	huffy	attempt	profligate
4.	**restive**	circular	oblong	sanctity	edgy	aloof
5.	**histrionic**	theatrical	consequent	absent	numerical	satirical
6.	**amalgam**	conclave	mixture	paunch	cased	concrete
7.	**ingenuous**	outlandish	floundering	bizarre	ultimate	naïve
8.	**antic**	disjoin	coax	guide	tell off	frolic

B. Missing words

Choose the best word to complete the sentences.

Most of us have heard about the mythical creature, the unicorn. The history of the unicorn is fascinating. The creature was (1)_____(invited, evicted, depicted) in early Mesopotamian artworks and has been (2)_____(mentioned, spoke, tell) in tales from Greece, India, China, and more. The unicorn has a (3)_____(double, single, pinkish) horn on top of its head and is (4)_____(make, nice, said) to have mysterious and magical powers. Although there are many (5)_____(unicorns, varieties, shadows) of unicorn stories, their captivating power remains the same.

C. Antonyms

Pick the word that means the opposite or near opposite of the word provided.

1.	**ameliorate**	iota	dulcet	dismiss	aggravate	rouse
2.	**revel**	retain	plot	scribe	grieve	transpire
3.	**undermine**	sheer	sneer	bolster	catalyst	destroy
4.	**curb**	emancipate	free up	encourage	lever	dish up
5.	**disheveled**	unkempt	exempt	untidy	messy	tidy
6.	**conform**	abide	pair up	glue	stick to	deviate
7.	**entreasure**	keep	lose	lock up	lock away	treasure
8.	**grandeur**	insignificance	incredible	keep true	imaginative	marvelous

D. Idioms

Match each idiom to its meaning.

1. **Be a guinea pig**   a. Look ugly

2. **A little bird told me**   b. A ineffective or unsuccessful person or thing

3. **A leg up**   c. A subject for experiment

4. **A tall order**   d. A difficult task

5. **Sight for sore eyes**   e. An advantage

6. **Act one's age, not one's shoe size**   f. Used when a source cannot be revealed

7. **A lame duck**   g. Don't be immature

Set 39

A. Synonyms

Select the word that most closely matches the meaning of the word provided.

1.	**parsimony**	thrift	brutal	luxury	generous	affluent
2.	**torpor**	botany	apathy	empathy	stash	technically
3.	**deferential**	ill mannered	scampered	overworked	respectful	dismal
4.	**perfidy**	dishonesty	witted	acquit	blunt	sharp
5.	**critical**	skilled	observed	curving	metallic	censorious
6.	**modest**	incompetent	frivolous	chaotic	demure	collapsed
7.	**mawkish**	happy	sappy	branchy	pitchy	punchy
8.	**predilection**	responsible	provisional	recommend	fondness	wide

B. Fill in the blanks

Fill in the blanks from the words in the table below. There are two extra words you do not need.

expectancy	couscous	reigned	processed	curate	decipher	quarreled

1. The king _____ for a total of seven years and three days.

2. They _____ often because they had stark differences of opinions.

3. The life _____ of that beetle is shockingly only an hour!

4. The ancient writing system was difficult to _____.

5. _____ foods are among the unhealthiest.

C. Homophones and homographs

Homophones are two or more words having the same pronunciation but different spellings and meanings. Homographs are words which have the same spelling but different meanings.

From the list below, fill in the blanks.

prophet	profit	ring	knot	sign	not

1. A piece of jewelry   _____

2. Write one's signature   _____

3. Make more money   _____

4. Make a clear and resonant sound   _____

5. A tied piece of thread, rope or similar   _____

6. A proclaimer of God   _____

7. A negative clause   _____

8. A notice   _____

D. Synonyms - Spelling

Complete the synonym of the word in **bold**.

1. **mainstream**   c __ __ m o n

2. **allow**   __ e r m __ __

3. **makeshift**   t __ __ p o r a r y

4. **ground-breaking**   i __ __ o v __ t i v e

5. **grueling**   s __ __ e r e

6. **revolt**   r __ __ e l

7. **crawl**   c __ __ e p

Set 40

A. Synonyms

Select the word that most closely matches the meaning of the word provided.

1.	**insubordinate**	abide	snide	concerned	rebellious	travesty
2.	**murmur**	shout	giggle	fight	whisper	turn
3.	**multifarious**	diverse	direct	indirect	close	intrepid
4.	**luxuriant**	lush	rush	grudge	fudge	ugly
5.	**emasculate**	undermine	determine	transform	stage	bolster
6.	**cranny**	crane	hangar	fan	pedicure	crevice
7.	**classification**	clause	grammar	juxtapose	category	tool
8.	**cladding**	covering	cleaner	hotel	building	plumbing

B. Missing words

Choose the best word to complete the sentences.

Claustrophobia is a common fear throughout the world. People who (1)_____(emaciate,

suffer, dwell) from claustrophobia have a fear of being in a (2)_____(confined,

confidential, confidantes) space. When (3)_____(confront, confronted, confused) with

their fear, sufferers can have panic attacks. However, some people can

(4)_____(overwhelm, overbear, overcome) their fear by seeing a

(5)_____(orthodontist, specialist, fundamentalist).

C. Antonyms

Pick the word that means the opposite or near opposite of the word provided.

1.	**prescience**	preemptive	innocent	hostile	finished	menacing
2.	**chortle**	enthuse	clairvoyant	claw	sob	cleanse
3.	**mitigate**	entwine	aggravate	entomb	iterate	itemize
4.	**subsume**	exclude	italicize	include	encompass	oblige
5.	**panache**	sludge	smelter	dither	obstruct	backward
6.	**spurious**	bogus	specious	sham	propagate	real
7.	**fallacious**	necessary	navel	prompt	correct	prophetic
8.	**elucidate**	meddling	invoice	confuse	invade	egomaniac

D. Idioms

Match each idiom to its meaning.

1. **After one's heart** a. Make someone feel worse when they are already feeling bad

2. **All eyes and ears** b. Be treated as you have done to others

3. **One trick pony** c. Be attentive

4. **Rub salt in the wound** d. Identify what others are thinking about a situation

5. **See which way the wind is blowing** e. Someone with only one talent

6. **Agree to disagree** f. Stop a disagreement and accept that neither party will change their view

7. **A taste of your own medicine** g. Having the same view or tastes

Set 41

A. Synonyms

Select the word that most closely matches the meaning of the word provided.

1.	**blatant**	deferential	cognitive	modest	glaring	procedure
2.	**ignoble**	beatified	confer	mean	gilded	privation
3.	**profane**	indirect	divorcee	commotion	soppy	impious
4.	**sham**	proactive	fictitious	whet	fortify	likened
5.	**largesse**	magnanimity	subdued	popular	desultory	crescendo
6.	**espouse**	adopt	serendipity	reject	oppose	ironed out
7.	**bumbling**	prism	lax	clumsy	ameliorate	prologue
8.	**pundit**	recrudescent	dysmorphia	savant	pranked	dumbfound

B. Fill in the blanks

Fill in the blanks from the words in the table below. There are two extra words you do not need.

egalitarian	effeminate	porous	piping	escapade	masticate	editorial

1. His views were strongly _____ and he wanted equal rights for all.

2. The _____ team decided to cancel the publication.

3. The eggshell was _____.

4. His long hair and earrings made him appear _____.

5. The espresso was _____ hot and delicious.

C. Homophones and homographs

Homophones are two or more words having the same pronunciation but different spellings and meanings. Homographs are words which have the same spelling but different meanings.

From the list below, fill in the blanks.

brew	pipe	stationery	laps	stationary	lapse

1. Boil, cook   _____

2. A drink   _____

3. Pens, paper, pencils   _____

4. Lengths of a pool, track   _____

5. A smoking tool   _____

6. Not moving   _____

7. A passage of time   _____

8. Used for transporting fluid   _____

D. Synonyms - Spelling

Complete the synonym of the word in **bold**.

1. **soar**   i __ __ r e a s e

2. **errand**   t __ __ k

3. **somber**   g __ __ __ m y

4. **dearth**   __ __ s e n c e

5. **colossal**   g __ __ n t

6. **whimsical**   e __ __ e n __ r i c

7. **heartfelt**   s __ __ c e r e

Set 42

A. Synonyms

Select the word that most closely matches the meaning of the word provided.

1.	**burgeon**	flourish	engrave	enslave	silvered	province
2.	**myopic**	territorial	originated	shortsighted	applicate	astronomer
3.	**bravado**	headband	quorum	bluster	quilt	rust
4.	**angst**	rustle	hustle	crevice	purify	anguish
5.	**cloying**	mildew	midwife	relax	remedy	saccharine
6.	**glib**	peeling	slick	migraine	edition	dunked
7.	**omen**	presage	jingoism	pneumatic	canvas	innate
8.	**gargantuan**	jeopardy	dormouse	orangutan	jumbo	puny

B. Missing words

Choose the best word to complete the sentences.

Laser is an (1)_____(moniker, acronym, name) meaning light amplification by stimulated emission of radiation. In these (2)_____(modern, presidential, carnivorous) times, lasers are used for amazing things. From the removal of (3)_____(wanting, unwanted, undoable) tattoos, to eye sight correction, scar reduction and engineering works, lasers are all around us and are (4)_____(utilitarianized, utilized, united) in unimaginable ways. The scientific research and (5)_____(studious, development, researching) of lasers promises even more fantastic things for the future.

C. Antonyms

Pick the word that means the opposite or near opposite of the word provided.

1.	**detoxify**	jobless	mummify	toxify	notify	verify
2.	**devious**	bicker	harmful	corrugated	sincere	resident
3.	**granular**	hoodwinked	poisonous	smooth	humiliated	humbled
4.	**due**	paid	turbulent	epicurean	verdant	golden
5.	**overstrung**	acidic	relaxed	impede	dreadful	gnarled
6.	**profound**	whet	distant	jerky	jocund	shallow
7.	**sophisticated**	urbane	matrilineal	newbie	uneducated	palisade
8.	**sonorous**	booming	quiet	loud	deep	resonant

D. Idioms

Match each idiom to its meaning.

1.	**Through thick and thin**	a. Cry a lot
2.	**Waste not, want not**	b. Start again
3.	**Back to the drawing board**	c. In difficult and easy times
4.	**Cry your eyes out**	d. Poor quality
5.	**Bottom of the barrel**	e. No longer in danger or difficulty
6.	**Out of the woods**	f. Time is valuable
7.	**Time is money**	g. Be resourceful, frugal

Set 43

A. Synonyms

Select the word that most closely matches the meaning of the word provided.

1.	**lurid**	dull	stifling	curt	stipend	sensational
2.	**Machiavelli**	exploitive	serene	declutter	consider	buzzing
3.	**paradox**	pox	limited	contradiction	timid	bulky
4.	**rustic**	crusty	crunchy	mural	epidural	rural
5.	**platitude**	cliché	melodic	niche	episodic	quiche
6.	**clamor**	commotion	clipped	bladed	blackthorn	masquerade
7.	**demagogue**	martyr	appeaser	listener	prong	troublemaker
8.	**cognizant**	oblivious	familiar	dissimilar	dissident	congruent

B. Fill in the blanks

Fill in the blanks from the words in the table below. There are two extra words you do not need.

restraint	lethargy	bittersweet	palindrome	measure	blacksmith	liaison

1. The name Hannah is a _____.

2. The _____ of the student was apparent. He was falling asleep at his desk.

3. The _____ between the two companies was beneficial.

4. Numerous cost-cutting_____(s) had to be taken to make up for the financial damage.

5. The police urged the protesters to exercise _____.

C. Homophones and homographs

Homophones are two or more words having the same pronunciation but different spellings and meanings. Homographs are words which have the same spelling but different meanings.

From the list below, fill in the blanks.

real	screen	cord	reel	chord	cry

1.   To produce tears when happy or sad   _____

2.   A roll of film   _____

3.   A musical note   _____

4.   Not a fantasy   _____

5.   To examine someone to check for the presence of disease   _____

6.   Scream or shout   _____

7.   A partition   _____

8.   String or rope   _____

D. Synonyms - Spelling

Complete the synonym of the word in **bold**.

1. **forecast**   p __ __ d i c t

2. **tainted**   t __ __ n __ __ h e d

3. **shovel**   s p __ __ e

4. **marquee**   t __ __ t

5. **rectitude**   i __ __ e g __ i t y

6. **flinch**   __ __ __ c e

7. **buyer**   s __ __ p p e r

Set 44

A. Synonyms

Select the word that most closely matches the meaning of the word provided.

1.	**brainstorm**	inscrutable	insatiate	plan	infatuate	lead
2.	**irony**	inshore	inquietude	satire	nicotine	neutron
3.	**meticulous**	puberty	rusticate	provincial	slovenly	careful
4.	**norm**	rule	anomaly	inset	worries	zany
5.	**plethora**	zygote	surplus	zilch	oomph	ongoing
6.	**virtual**	contradict	frenetic	capable	simulated	tangible
7.	**scrutinize**	capitally	inanimate	examine	zircon	overman
8.	**plagiarize**	zebu	scour	steal	sciatic	palatial

B. Missing words

Choose the best word to complete the sentences.

The hadal zone, also referred to as the hadopelagic zone, is the (1)_____(most deep, deepest, intresingest) part of the ocean. It (2)_____(liars, lies, lyes) beneath the abyssal zone at depths that are greater than 6,000m (19,500 ft.). The hadal zone is where ocean trenches are (3)_____(situationed, stationed, situated). The pressure in the hadal zone is six thousand times greater than the (4)_____(bombastic, atmospheric, posthumous) pressure around us. Unsurprisingly, the zone is so deep that there is no (5)_____(marine, trench, light).

C. Antonyms

Pick the word that means the opposite or near opposite of the word provided.

1.	**articulate**	glib	shadowy	taciturn	turbo	vinous
2.	**domestic**	pigsty	supplicate	public	shade	viewfinder
3.	**corroborate**	affirm	turbine	brambles	deny	stirrer
4.	**feeble**	strong	tuckered	pen	perennial	stink
5.	**covered**	leafy	bare	showplace	prerecord	layered
6.	**gravitate**	philately	partisan	nonplussed	moonlit	retreat
7.	**incite**	shambles	monstrous	pacify	focal	eerie
8.	**inoculate**	infect	nonchalant	inject	extrovert	vaccinate

D. Idioms

Match each idiom to its meaning.

1. **Change one's tune**   a. Ruin someone's pleasure or enthusiasm

2. **Rain on someone's parade**   b. Use the toilet

3. **Powder one's nose**   c. Make a mistake when the task is easy

4. **Nothing to write home about**   d. Be in charge

5. **In someone's neck of the woods**   e. Change one's mind

6. **Rookie error**   f. Ordinary

7. **Rule the roost**   g. In someone's familiar area

Set 45

A. Synonyms

Select the word that most closely matches the meaning of the word provided.

1.	**circuitous**	straight	indirect	tropical	redemption	recoup
2.	**impute**	ascribe	dormant	protract	emancipate	emulate
3.	**subtle**	murky	artifact	undermine	delicate	boisterous
4.	**rancorous**	equivocal	offset	effeminate	impeccable	bitter
5.	**repeat**	nines	perpetual	conceptual	peevish	saddle
6.	**indoctrinate**	wretch	drill	liberate	put up	sadden
7.	**iconic**	stench	emblematic	recurring	make do	mundane
8.	**throttle**	stroke	outlandish	choke	sack	throat

B. Fill in the blanks

Fill in the blanks from the words in the table below. There are two extra words you do not need.

flex	divorcee	domineering	flog	devoid	harmonize	dossier

1. The convict was on the stand, _____ of all emotion.

2. The _____ hoped to find a new partner worthy of marriage.

3. The _____ sat neatly amongst other paperwork and books.

4. The ruthless king was very _____.

5. The school choir could _____ even the most difficult of songs.

C. Homophones and homographs

Homophones are two or more words having the same pronunciation but different spellings and meanings. Homographs are words which have the same spelling but different meanings.

From the list below, fill in the blanks.

lava	novel	idol	larva	idle	tear

1. Molten rock   _____

2. Lazy   _____

3. A book   _____

4. Rip   _____

5. A maggot   _____

6. Interestingly original   _____

7. A _____ drop   _____

8. Someone you look up to   _____

D. Synonyms - Spelling

Complete the synonym of the word in **bold**.

1. **lacerate**   t __ __ r

2. **endurance**   __ __ a m i n a

3. **effort**   e __ __ t i o n

4. **vicinity**   n __ __ r __ e s s

5. **mariner**   s __ __ l __ __

6. **margin**   e __ g __

7. **refurbish**   r __ __ o v __ __ e

Set 46

A. Synonyms

Select the word that most closely matches the meaning of the word provided.

1.	**sullen**	hazy	authority	morose	questions	parole
2.	**flummox**	confound	accurate	proviso	wane	loving
3.	**ineffable**	caricature	animalistic	captivate	arguable	unutterable
4.	**incendiary**	supple	medical	demagogue	arsonist	obvious
5.	**noxious**	benign	anodyne	teeters	sanitize	injurious
6.	**infatuate**	militate	captivate	cultivate	capture	midriff
7.	**accumulate**	accrue	progressive	demonstrate	oblige	express
8.	**sanguine**	insensate	upbeat	reinstate	offbeat	unhand

B. Missing words

Choose the best word to complete the sentences.

Aristotle is a well-known philosopher. His ideas and works are still (1)_____(prevalent, preaching, resident) to this day. College seminars, hobbyists, and filmmakers often use his ideas to their advantage. Aristotle was a (2)_____(treacherous, student, bud) of another one of the great (3)_____(teachings, discussions, philosophers), Plato. Although Aristotle is so famous, even all these years later, very (4)_____(minute, small, little) is known about his life. (5)_____(irrelevant, regardless, recoupering) of this fact, his legacy still lives on.

C. Antonyms

Pick the word that means the opposite or near opposite of the word provided.

1.	**partisan**	innards	unbiased	economic	mollusk	molecular
2.	**heckle**	extol	content	abolish	solidify	trump
3.	**ignoble**	filthy	falsify	innovate	honorable	ignorable
4.	**literate**	laudatory	trellis	latchkey	missive	ignorant
5.	**evince**	evidence	avidness	camouflage	lyricism	frack
6.	**engender**	missile	barky	crush	remote	padding
7.	**bona fide**	bogus	oxymoron	rendezvous	pack in	lading
8.	**attenuate**	expand	lacquered	hock	hobnob	fusible

D. Idioms

Match each idiom to its meaning.

1.	**No rhyme or reason**	a. Something specially annoying to someone
2.	**Not cut out for**	b. To be very similar
3.	**Pet peeve**	c. Lessen the intensity of something unpleasant
4.	**Swim with sharks**	d. No logic behind the action
5.	**Take the edge off**	e. Extremely inexpensive
6.	**Cut from the same cloth**	f. To operate among dangerous people
7.	**Dime a dozen**	g. Not be equipped for

Set 47

A. Synonyms

Select the word that most closely matches the meaning of the word provided.

1. **raconteur**   lotus   storyteller   bogus   gatekeeper   quizzer

2. **nemesis**   enemy   witch   minder   pet   argument

3. **lithe**   publisher   newsagent   timber   limber   wooden

4. **sumptuous**   tumultuous   permit   decipher   plush   clique

5. **ebullience**   belie   enthrall   cursory   accented   vivacity

6. **mendacity**   wounded   monopoly   falsehood   gainsay   ginger

7. **evince**   somnolence   reveal   humanity   brisk   bristly

8. **holistic**   gripe   integrated   moped   boastful   decrepit

B. Fill in the blanks

Fill in the blanks from the words in the table below. There are two extra words you do not need.

consecutive	loveless	foolhardy	gnomic	gradation	grievous	consternation

1. The feeling of _____ was crippling.

2. The _____ of the artwork was simply beautiful.

3. Although they were stuck in a _____ relationship, there was no hostility between them.

4. The _____ actions of the youth landed them in prison.

5. The weather has been dry for three _____ months.

C. Homophones and homographs

Homophones are two or more words having the same pronunciation but different spellings and meanings. Homographs are words which have the same spelling but different meanings.

From the list below, fill in the blanks.

you'll	spirit	yule	address	woe	whoa

1.   You will   _____

2.   An expression of shock, delight   _____

3.   The soul, a ghost   _____

4.   Sadness or distress   _____

5.   Christmas time   _____

6.   Where a person lives   _____

7.   Speak to people   _____

8.   Alcoholic drink   _____

D. Synonyms - Spelling

Complete the synonym of the word in **bold**.

1. **apropos**   f ___ ___ t i n g

2. **lunatic**   c ___ ___ ___ y

3. **grandiose**   i ___ ___ r ___ s s i v e

4. **elegant**   g ___ ___ c e f ___ l

5. **path**   p a ___ ___ a g e

6. **impact**   ___ f f e c t

7. **recruit**   e ___ r ___ l l

Set 48

A. Synonyms

Select the word that most closely matches the meaning of the word provided.

1.	**bamboozle**	suffice	assist	chosen	bashful	deceive
2.	**deleterious**	gatecrash	professor	certain	harmful	sneak around
3.	**salubrious**	breakable	nunnery	machinery	healthy	moisten
4.	**anodyne**	narcotic	behemoth	baneful	bejeweled	baleful
5.	**pundit**	chevron	expert	secret	muddle	mull over
6.	**prehensile**	noodle	nondescript	grasping	tippled	nuzzle
7.	**tedium**	medium	bizarreness	vow	absent	dreariness
8.	**atrophied**	tempest	hothead	bailed	wasted	violent

B. Missing words

Choose the best word to complete the sentences.

Collagen is a protein that our bodies (1)_____(quick, painstakingly, naturally) make. It is a protein that helps our body to repair tissue. Due to the (2)_____(tyranny, boldness, power) that collagen has, many skincare brands have jumped on the collagen (3)_____(bus, bandwagon, train) and are fortifying products with collagen.

The companies (4)_____(shop, supermarket, market) their products as skin saviors. However, many scientists have argued that unless an (5)_____(all round, all ground, all done) healthy lifestyle is maintained, there is only so much that these collagen supplements and products can do.

C. Antonyms

Pick the word that means the opposite or near opposite of the word provided.

1.	**constrained**	independent	nominal	sticky	frivolous	lumpy
2.	**inferior**	choice	node	noiseless	mélange	brewed
3.	**discrepancy**	jerkin	elision	perfection	jeopardize	melancholy
4.	**thundering**	peaceful	detrimental	loud	dollop	domed
5.	**apace**	consecrate	bauble	beagle	embittered	tardily
6.	**privation**	want	penury	opulence	indigence	destitution
7.	**blithely**	paralytic	dolefully	parable	pious	pinhole
8.	**heedfully**	pinnace	plowshare	pinnacle	undisguised	inadvertently

D. Idioms

Match each idiom to its meaning.

1.	**Till the cows come home**	a. To change one's mind constantly
2.	**Blow hot and cold**	b. Something is not done well if too many people become involved
3.	**Too many cooks spoil the broth**	c. A heavy workload
4.	**Up to one's neck**	d. An unending negative situation
5.	**Vicious circle**	e. Stop being involved
6.	**Wash your hands of**	f. Industrious and enthusiastic
7.	**Eager Beaver**	g. For an indefinitely long time

Set 49

A. Synonyms

Select the word that most closely matches the meaning of the word provided.

1.	**miraculous**	dictated	wondrous	further	usual	mundane
2.	**threadbare**	worn	pristine	opulent	pristine	bling
3.	**abjure**	bright	microscopic	renounce	lethargic	casted
4.	**aberration**	suspicious	anomaly	suited	innuendo	crescendo
5.	**bungalow**	town	city	joyous	dwelling	viscous
6.	**abject**	yielding	wretched	extravagant	paramount	authority
7.	**misanthrope**	fielding	ruler	extroverted	moved	cynic
8.	**subterfuge**	compatible	bile	compadre	composted	ploy

B. Fill in the blanks

Fill in the blanks from the words in the table below. There are two extra words you do not need.

scripture	dictate	edible	irrevocably	immune	efface	crux

1. My life changed _____ after the serious accident.

2. Super humans will be _____ to diseases.

3. His coping mechanism was to _____ the difficult memories from his mind.

4. The followers take the words spoken to them as _____.

5. "You don't _____ what I do!" The boy shouted to his mother.

C. Homophones and homographs

Homophones are two or more words having the same pronunciation but different spellings and meanings. Homographs are words which have the same spelling but different meanings.

From the list below, fill in the blanks.

bag	roar	world	rebel	raw	whirled

1. A hold all   _____

2. Uncooked   _____

3. Fight back against authority   _____

4. The sound made by big cats   _____

5. The earth, together with everything on it   _____

6. Succeed in securing something   _____

7. Spun around   _____

8. Laugh loudly   _____

D. Synonyms - Spelling

Complete the synonym of the word in **bold**.

1. **plant life**   f __ __ r a

2. **ruffle**   u __ s e t t l __

3. **jargon**   __ __ a n g

4. **mill**   __ __ i n d e

5. **morass**   q __ __ g m i __ e

6. **panacea**   r __ m e d __

7. **plaudit**   a __ __ l a i m

Set 50

A. Synonyms

Select the word that most closely matches the meaning of the word provided.

1.	**scintilla**	iota	constraint	complaint	rod	rote
2.	**mellifluous**	deafening	magnify	dulcet	spectacle	frosty
3.	**repeat**	confident	sieved	gloomy	nimble	unattractive
4.	**axiom**	peaceful	maxim	brew	bullish	sanitizer
5.	**surreptitious**	futuristic	quince	transparent	furtive	wasteful
6.	**eloquence**	deity	reliability	monotint	yappy	fluency
7.	**taciturn**	public	reserved	congealed	mistaken	immaculate
8.	**insolent**	brazen	brewed	prepared	idle	corrugated

B. Missing words

Choose the best word to complete the sentences.

Gone are the days of college majors being limited. The (1)_____(box, selection, select) of courses on offer is vast. From the weird and wonderful, to the more traditional, and everything in between. There is something on offer for all. If you're a (2)_____(pendulous, prance, proficient) baker, baking science might be your (3)_____(gratin, go, forte). A history lover? Then why not (4)_____(read, studious, yelp) history? Whatever you choose, college is (5)_____(obtrusive, exclusive, inclusive) and there is something for everyone to enjoy!

C. Antonyms

Pick the word that means the opposite or near opposite of the word provided.

1.	**disgruntled**	shot	contented	terminate	obvious	conceive
2.	**conciliate**	rhyme	agitate	ribaldry	pique	piping
3.	**atone**	dismiss	expiate	fared	repaginate	pious
4.	**querulous**	waning	dithered	evolved	affable	evoke
5.	**aromatic**	withered	diverged	divided	pivot	odorless
6.	**misunderstand**	avert	pioneer	divest	combust	assimilate
7.	**allot**	spiced	faded	established	monkey	retain
8.	**savant**	sage	expert	pundit	ignoramus	imperial

D. Idioms

Match each idiom to its meaning.

1.	**Back on one's feet**	a. A long time
2.	**All the rage**	b. Likely
3.	**Second wind**	c. Not complicated or challenging
4.	**In a month of Sundays**	d. The natural world
5.	**Ten to one**	e. In fashion
6.	**Like shooting fish in a barrel**	f. Feeling better after being down
7.	**Mother nature**	g. A new burst of energy after being exhausted

Answers

Set 1: Answers

A. Synonyms

1. quiet	2. incarcerate	3. cunning	4. revere	5. abstruse
6. determined	7. heartless	8. destructive		

B. Fill in the blanks

1. barter	2. detest	3. frugal	4. avert	5. amicable

C. Homographs

1. sure	2. shore	3. frequent	4. stair	5. frequent
6. minute	7. minute	8. stare		

D. Synonyms - Spelling

1. shape	2. smug	3. scrutinize	4. patient	5. jocular
6. combine	7. corrupt			

Set 2: Answers

A. Synonyms

1. rich	2. opposition	3. haphazard	4. slow	5. annoyance
6. berate	7. violent	8. integrity		

B. Missing Words

1. multitude	2. bizarre	3. formidable	4. tedious	5. fainthearted

C. Antonyms

1. special	2. welcome	3. virtue	4. appease	5. intangible
6. member	7. allow	8. conceal		

D. Idioms

1. e	2. b	3. d	4. a	5. f
6. c	7. g			

Set 3: Answers

A. Synonyms

1. warn	2. energetic	3. bitter	4. praise	5. loiter
6. eradicate	7. confuse	8. obstruct		

B. Fill in the blanks

1. pristine	2. erratic	3. meander	4. viscous	5. aspire

C. Homographs

1. May	2. blue	3. hall	4. birth	5. haul
6. blue	7. may	8. berth		

D. Synonyms - Spelling

1. bold	2. honesty	3. rude	4. nerve	5. diagnosis
6. cool	7. careful			

Set 4: Answers

A. Synonyms

1. endurance	2. reject	3. obdurate	4. mad	5. ordinary
6. garrulous	7. tyranny	8. vilify		

B. Missing Words

1. commonly	2. produce	3. roles	4. head	5. crucial

C. Antonyms

1. joyful	2. apathetic	3. confirm	4. corrupting	5. freedom
6. arid	7. enhance	8. fair		

D. Idioms

1. d	2. b	3. f	4. c	5. g
6. e	7. a			

Set 5: Answers

A. Synonyms

1. skill	2. tirade	3. booth	4. shout	5. edge
6. wrong	7. disprove	8. collection		

B. Fill in the blanks

1. hardy	2. recoil	3. expiate	4. raze	5. prologue

C. Homographs

1. principal	2. bank	3. weigh	4. principle	5. bank
6. letter	7. way	8. letter		

D. Synonyms - Spelling

1. trash	2. cunning	3. hostile	4. wandering	5. budding
6. resident	7. peak			

Set 6: Answers

A. Synonyms

1. wipe out	2. passion	3. harmless	4. quick	5. desire
6. begin	7. period	8. bicker		

B. Missing Words

1. notable	2. copious	3. poems	4. legacy	5. works

C. Antonyms

1. alacrity	2. constant	3. mature	4. flourish	5. tight
6. contentment	7. receiver	8. aggravate		

D. Idioms

1. f	2. c	3. g	4. e	5. b
6. d	7. a			

Set 7: Answers

A. Synonyms

1. revoke
2. enthusiasm
3. solution
4. prevent
5. breeze
6. ridicule
7. posture
8. plead

B. Fill in the blanks

1. vapid
2. urbane
3. desultory
4. voracious
5. crescendo

C. Homographs

1. resume
2. nail
3. dew
4. sweet
5. suite
6. nail
7. resume
8. due

D. Synonyms - Spelling

1. lethargic
2. cover
3. grand
4. taint
5. loot
6. warning
7. diminish

Set 8: Answers

A. Synonyms

1. reinforce
2. sharpen
3. desire
4. clumsy
5. subdue
6. lively
7. urge
8. decline

B. Missing Words

1. popular
2. countries
3. unique
4. traditionally
5. try

C. Antonyms

1. cynical
2. harsh
3. determined
4. respectable
5. continuous
6. graceful
7. scarcity
8. well

D. Idioms

1. e
2. a
3. g
4. c
5. b
6. d
7. f

Set 9: Answers

A. Synonyms

1. golden	2. poisonous	3. city	4. conceited	5. uniform
6. support	7. prohibited	8. annoyance		

B. Fill in the blanks

1. associate	2. accomplice	3. hoodwink	4. epicurean	5. dialect

C. Homographs

1. wine	2. entrance	3. down	4. core	5. whine
6. corps	7. down	8. entrance		

D. Synonyms - Spelling

1. peculiarity	2. uneducated	3. occasional	4. give	5. annoy
6. adept	7. incisive			

Set 10: Answers

A. Synonyms

1. reproach	2. useful	3. eradicate	4. priesthood	5. ragamuffin
6. rude	7. sycophant	8. deadly		

B. Missing Words

1. deadliest	2. whopping	3. only	4. alive	5. repellent

C. Antonyms

1. practical	2. kind	3. quiet	4. serious	5. unsociable
6. love	7. sociable	8. rich		

D. Idioms

1. g	2. b	3. f	4. e	5. d
6. a	7. c			

Set 11: Answers

A. Synonyms

1. split	2. scale	3. sturdy	4. expert	5. justifiable
6. breakable	7. inexperienced	8. store		

B. Fill in the blanks

1. authentic	2. resilience	3. analogy	4. placate	5. inundate

C. Homographs

1. guest	2. extract	3. nose	4. contract	5. knows
6. contract	7. guessed	8. extract		

D. Synonyms - Spelling

1. neutral	2. creator	3. argument	4. food	5. district
6. drunk	7. flexible			

Set 12: Answers

A. Synonyms

1. annoyance	2. lingo	3. jolly	4. result	5. erratic
6. city	7. angelic	8. fortress		

B. Missing Words

1. famous	2. confirmed	3. speculating	4. extortionate	5. auction

C. Antonyms

1. conceal	2. neglect	3. temporary	4. destroy	5. indifferent
6. restrained	7. create	8. solution		

D. Idioms

1. b	2. e	3. a	4. f	5. d
6. g	7. c			

Set 13: Answers

A. Synonyms

1. defer	2. strengthen	3. foreign	4. ruse	5. banishment
6. quip	7. fruitful	8. precise		

B. Fill in the blanks

1. semblance	2. daunting	3. pilfer	4. surmount	5. adherent

C. Homographs

1. digest	2. coward	3. morn	4. digest	5. mourn
6. desert	7. cowered	8. desert		

D. Synonyms - Spelling

1. stimulant	2. incurable	3. veiled	4. assertive	5. drivel
6. refute	7. rebuke			

Set 14: Answers

A. Synonyms

1. subjugation	2. haphazard	3. inactive	4. fund	5. impede
6. cut	7. afflicted	8. eerie		

B. Missing Words

1. cultivated	2. wild	3. prefers	4. acidic	5. tolerant

C. Antonyms

1. wealthy	2. simple	3. informal	4. unclear	5. polite
6. essential	7. deny	8. applaud		

D. Idioms

1. b	2. g	3. e	4. c	5. f
6. d	7. a			

Set 15: Answers

A. Synonyms

1. thoughtful	2. dangerous	3. inferior	4. agile	5. dour
6. enlarge	7. transient	8. guarantee		

B. Fill in the blanks

1. immunity	2. flippant	3. dross	4. institute	5. pugnacious

C. Homographs

1. agape	2. axes	3. we've	4. axes	5. weave
6. mown	7. moan	8. agape		

D. Synonyms - Spelling

1. reimburse	2. meager	3. excellent	4. risk	5. twist
6. accessory	7. honest			

Set 16: Answers

A. Synonyms

1. toil	2. delegate	3. breed	4. enslave	5. burn
6. untwine	7. cliff	8. mock-up		

B. Missing Words

1. paramount	2. comprehensive	3. pernicious	4. avoid	5. exposure

C. Antonyms

1. stiff	2. praise	3. ordinary	4. calm	5. safe
6. soothe	7. true	8. active		

D. Idioms

1. e	2. c	3. a	4. g	5. b
6. d	7. f			

Set 17: Answers

A. Synonyms

1. abuse	2. spoil	3. provide	4. doubtful	5. bulletproof
6. rough	7. botched	8. offhand		

B. Fill in the blanks

1. exquisite	2. interact	3. intrepid	4. latent	5. blatant

C. Homographs

1. chair	2. choral	3. latter	4. coordinate	5. coral
6. coordinate	7. ladder	8. chair		

D. Synonyms - Spelling

1. eradicate	2. respect	3. mock	4. bemused	5. immensity
6. actual	7. brazen			

Set 18: Answers

A. Synonyms

1. acquit	2. thwart	3. jumble	4. advocate	5. trill
6. flinch	7. ruthless	8. gully		

B. Missing Words

1. invasive	2. destruction	3. smuggled	4. causing	5. leading

C. Antonyms

1. sophisticated	2. apathy	3. clarify	4. allay	5. veto
6. composed	7. validate	8. fail		

D. Idioms

1. f	2. d	3. a	4. b	5. c
6. g	7. e			

Set 19: Answers

A. Synonyms

1. genial	2. aggressive	3. flatter	4. benefit	5. repression
6. hypocrisy	7. briskness	8. barrier		

B. Fill in the blanks

1. topically	2. anesthetic	3. beguile	4. buoyant	5. absolute

C. Homographs

1. moped	2. oh	3. wind	4. owe	5. wind
6. moped	7. addition	8. edition		

D. Synonyms - Spelling

1. devious	2. drunken	3. misuse	4. obscure	5. rumor
6. boastful	7. confused			

Set 20: Answers

A. Synonyms

1. benevolent	2. eminent	3. capricious	4. maximum	5. slow
6. divide	7. stupor	8. cogitate		

B. Missing Words

1. throng	2. wander	3. inquire	4. invite	5. astounded

C. Antonyms

1. outflow	2. flush	3. extricate	4. extol	5. dissuade
6. keep	7. accept	8. intemperate		

D. Idioms

1. b	2. e	3. a	4. f	5. c
6. g	7. d			

Set 21: Answers

A. Synonyms

1. reunite	2. judicious	3. motto	4. pretentious	5. unbeliever
6. challenge	7. jocular	8. moniker		

B. Fill in the blanks

1. bibliophile	2. dwelling	3. euphemism	4. ingenious	5. articulate

C. Homographs

1. break	2. too	3. console	4. to	5. brake
6. crane	7. console	8. crane		

D. Synonyms - Spelling

1. die	2. douse	3. isolate	4. firm	5. verify
6. academic	7. disputable			

Set 22: Answers

A. Synonyms

1. democratic	2. fearless	3. inferno	4. coax	5. arrogate
6. sheepishly	7. bond	8. eternity		

B. Missing Words

1. shown	2. handy	3. addictive	4. excruciating	5. monitor

C. Antonyms

1. save	2. legato	3. negligible	4. democratic	5. color
6. reverence	7. individual	8. surrender		

D. Idioms

1. e	2. f	3. d	4. b	5. a
6. g	7. c			

Set 23: Answers

A. Synonyms

1. iniquitous	2. sentimental	3. tolerant	4. inherent	5. atrocious
6. salvo	7. audacity	8. distrustful		

B. Fill in the blanks

1. pontificate	2. critter	3. eloquent	4. attitude	5. ingénue

C. Homographs

1. drape	2. capital	3. compliment	4. drape	5. lead
6. complement	7. capitol	8. lead		

D. Synonyms - Spelling

1. perfect	2. truant	3. recovery	4. law	5. dismay
6. essence	7. infused			

Set 24: Answers

A. Synonyms

1. heavenly	2. pungent	3. cruel	4. stopover	5. annul
6. tinge	7. primitive	8. afraid		

B. Missing Words

1. magnificent	2. research	3. findings	4. pressure	5. allergy

C. Antonyms

1. unlettered	2. dwindle	3. calm	4. impotent	5. legitimate
6. noble	7. commoner	8. giggle		

D. Idioms

1. f	2. g	3. a	4. e	5. b
6. c	7. d			

Set 25: Answers

A. Synonyms

1. outer	2. harden	3. hazy	4. vortex	5. suspicious
6. scheme	7. courageous	8. authority		

B. Fill in the blanks

1. depleted	2. mutiny	3. docile	4. miserly	5. nepotism

C. Homographs

1. banned	2. mayor	3. mare	4. band	5. sewer
6. wound	7. sewer	8. wound		

D. Synonyms - Spelling

1. custom	2. speech	3. biased	4. per person	5. passive
6. monotony	7. parole			

Set 26: Answers

A. Synonyms

1. parody	2. edge	3. decline	4. abstinence	5. rosy
6. defiant	7. idealistic	8. condition		

B. Missing Words

1. substance	2. loving	3. plumper	4. grotesque	5. staple

C. Antonyms

1. sharp	2. passionate	3. dirty	4. fortunate	5. emotional
6. explanation	7. romantic	8. shun		

D. Idioms

1. e	2. a	3. d	4. f	5. g
6. c	7. b			

Set 27: Answers

A. Synonyms

1. itinerant	2. idle	3. ebullient	4. revelation	5. opaque
6. hasty	7. spoil	8. opulent		

B. Fill in the blanks

1. strenuous	2. trounce	3. temerity	4. apprised	5. tenuous

C. Homographs

1. back	2. stork	3. stalk	4. steak	5. accent
6. accent	7. back	8. stake		

D. Synonyms - Spelling

1. fierce	2. petty	3. sully	4. valid	5. ardent
6. juicy	7. mental			

Set 28: Answers

A. Synonyms

1. brief	2. submit	3. roll	4. patronize	5. set free
6. lecturer	7. low	8. monarch		

B. Missing Words

1. residing	2. minute	3. microscope	4. perturbed	5. slightest

C. Antonyms

1. conformity	2. light	3. unstylish	4. raised	5. equals
6. generous	7. valid	8. altruistic		

D. Idioms

1. c	2. e	3. g	4. b	5. d
6. a	7. f			

Set 29: Answers

A. Synonyms

1. economical	2. penniless	3. hazy	4. fleeting	5. covetous
6. agree	7. truculent	8. hoard		

B. Fill in the blanks

1. bogus	2. chimerical	3. congeal	4. fallible	5. fathom

C. Homographs

1. chest	2. jeans	3. watt	4. genes	5. chest
6. cock	7. what	8. cock		

D. Synonyms - Spelling

1. cupidity	2. hit	3. complain	4. humanitarian	5. garden
6. reward	7. multilingual			

Set 30: Answers

A. Synonyms

1. avarice	2. roomy	3. discreet	4. gripping	5. affluent
6. pierce	7. compact	8. cranky		

B. Missing Words

1. layman's	2. stems	3. feat	4. attributes	5. prosper

C. Antonyms

1. announce	2. defiant	3. accept	4. harmful	5. dawdle
6. reject	7. support	8. enemy		

D. Idioms

1. f	2. c	3. a	4. b	5. g
6. e	7. d			

Set 31: Answers

A. Synonyms

1. gather	2. theoretical	3. shame	4. treacherous	5. augur
6.leading	7. greedy	8. prohibit		

B. Fill in the blanks

1. linchpin	2. verdant	3. wheedling	4. sagacious	5. egregious

C. Homographs

1. pedal	2. pie	3. fall	4. pi	5. content
6. peddle	7. fall	8. content		

D. Synonyms - Spelling

1. thoughtful	2. brackets	3.violation	4. beg	5. pellucid
6. forefront	7. vexation			

Set 32: Answers

A. Synonyms

1. captive	2. needy	3. exhaustion	4. fetid	5. mollify
6. slander	7. oppose	8. drudge		

B. Missing Words

1. arguably	2. improving	3. abstaining	4. nevertheless	5. draw

C. Antonyms

1. placate	2. usual	3. obvious	4.fervent	5. choice
6. join	7. individual	8. love		

D. Idioms

1. d	2. f	3. c	4. a	5. b
6. g	7. e			

Set 33: Answers

A. Synonyms

1.suppose	2. rebellion	3. proud	4. intense	5. candid
6. ductile	7. munificence	8. fascinate		

B. Fill in the blanks

1. iconoclastic	2. goosebumps	3. figurative	4. internecine	5. fleeting

C. Homographs

1. well	2. wave	3. horde	4. kernel	5. well
6. hoard	7. wave	8. colonel		

D. Synonyms - Spelling

1. farewell	2. perch	3. hesitant	4. incongruous	5. dazed
6. irregular	7. splinter			

Set 34: Answers

A. Synonyms

1. obsequious	2. bombastic	3. integrity	4. coarse	5. gather
6. arduous	7. hard up	8. repeat		

B. Missing Words

1. translates	2. represents	3. finest	4. fireworks	5. regions

C. Antonyms

1. maladroit	2. mild	3. colossal	4. interesting	5. degrade
6. kind	7. short	8. unmanned		

D. Idioms

1. e	2. g	3. c	4. a	5. b
6. d	7. f			

Set 35: Answers

A. Synonyms

1. varied	2. luck	3. charitable	4. fellowship	5. pernicious
6. cynical	7. ecstatic	8. alternate		

B. Fill in the blanks

1. axis	2. reason	3. exist	4. seasons	5. tremendously

C. Homographs

1. hanger	2. cruise	3. fast	4. float	5. crews
6. hangar	7. fast	8. float		

D. Synonyms - Spelling

1. throw away	2. sanctify	3. superficial	4. domain	5. measurement
6. province	7. copious			

Set 36: Answers

A. Synonyms

1. pressurize	2. stupefied	3. take	4. scheme	5. eager
6. voracious	7. scholarly	8. phony		

B. Missing Words

1. moves	2. kinds	3. diagonally	4. on the other hand	5. power

C. Antonyms

1. actual	2. active	3. modesty	4. idiocy	5.depression
6. work-shy	7. consistent	8. base		

D. Idioms

1. f	2. g	3. c	4. a	5. d
6. e	7. b			

Set 37: Answers

A. Synonyms

1. uncertain	2. precision	3. abbreviate	4. universal	5. composure
6. placid	7. jumpy	8. quirky		

B. Fill in the blanks

1. gargantuan	2. biodiversity	3. diseases	4. obliterated	5. coverage

C. Homographs

1. sent	2. we'd	3. implant	4. scent	5. match
6. weed	7. match	8. implant		

D. Synonyms - Spelling

1. orchard	2. signal	3. stoop	4. whack	5. gangster
6. forbidden	7. euphoria			

Set 38: Answers

A. Synonyms

1. irrelevant	2. inactive	3. profligate	4. edgy	5. theatrical
6. mixture	7. naive	8. frolic		

B. Missing Words

1. depicted	2. mentioned	3. single	4. said	5. varieties

C. Antonyms

1. aggravate	2. grieve	3. bolster	4. encourage	5. tidy
6. deviate	7. lose	8. insignificance		

D. Idioms

1. c	2. f	3. e	4. d	5. a
6. g	7. b			

Set 39: Answers

A. Synonyms

1. thrift	2. apathy	3. respectful	4. dishonesty	5. censorious
6. demure	7. sappy	8. fondness		

B. Fill in the blanks

1. reigned	2. quarreled	3. expectancy	4. decipher	5. processed

C. Homographs

1. ring	2. sign	3. profit	4. ring	5. knot
6. prophet	7. not	8. sign		

D. Synonyms - Spelling

1. common	2. permit	3. temporary	4. innovative	5. severe
6. rebel	7. creep			

Set 40: Answers

A. Synonyms

1. rebellious	2. whisper	3. diverse	4. lush	5. undermine
6. crevice	7. category	8. covering		

B. Missing Words

1. suffer	2. confined	3. confronted	4. overcome	5. specialist

C. Antonyms

1. finished	2. sob	3. aggravate	4. cession	5. backward
6. real	7. correct	8. confuse		

D. Idioms

1. g	2. c	3. e	4. a	5. d
6. f	7. b			

Set 41: Answers

A. Synonyms

1. glaring	2. mean	3. impious	4. fictitious	5. magnanimity
6. adopt	7. clumsy	8. savant		

B. Fill in the blanks

1. egalitarian	2. editorial	3. porous	4. effeminate	5. piping

C. Homographs

1. brew	2. brew	3. stationery	4. laps	5. pipe
6. stationary	7. lapse	8. pipe		

D. Synonyms - Spelling

1. increase	2. task	3. gloomy	4. absence	5. giant
6. eccentric	7. sincere			

Set 42: Answers

A. Synonyms

1. flourish	2. shortsighted	3. bluster	4. anguish	5. saccharine
6. slick	7. presage	8. jumbo		

B. Missing Words

1. acronym	2. modern	3. unwanted	4. utilized	5. development

C. Antonyms

1. toxify	2. sincere	3. smooth	4. paid	5. relaxed
6. shallow	7. uneducated	8. quiet		

D. Idioms

1. c	2. g	3. b	4. a	5. d
6. e	7. f			

Set 43: Answers

A. Synonyms

1. sensational   2. exploitive   3. contradiction   4. rural   5. cliché

6. commotion   7. troublemaker   8. familiar

B. Fill in the blanks

1. palindrome   2. lethargy   3. liaison   4. countermeasure   5. restraint

C. Homographs

1. cry   2. reel   3. chord   4. real   5. screen

6. cry   7. screen   8. cord

D. Synonyms - Spelling

1. predict   2. tarnished   3. spade   4. tent   5. integrity

6. wince   7. shopper

Set 44: Answers

A. Synonyms

1. plan   2. satire   3. careful   4. rule   5. surplus

6. simulated   7. examine   8. steal

B. Missing Words

1. deepest   2. lies   3. situated   4. atmospheric   5. light

C. Antonyms

1. taciturn   2. public   3. deny   4. strong   5. bare

6. retreat   7. pacify   8. infect

D. Idioms

1. e   2. a   3. b   4. f   5. g

6. c   7. d

Set 45: Answers

A. Synonyms

1. indirect	2. ascribe	3. delicate	4. bitter	5. peevish
6. drill	7. emblematic	8. choke		

B. Fill in the blanks

1. devoid	2. divorcee	3. dossier	4. domineering	5. harmonize

C. Homographs

1. lava	2. idle	3. novel	4. tear	5. larva
6. novel	7. tear	8. idol		

D. Synonyms - Spelling

1. tear	2. stamina	3. exertion	4. nearness	5. sailor
6. edge	7. renovate			

Set 46: Answers

A. Synonyms

1. morose	2. confound	3. unutterable	4. arsonist	5. injurious
6. captivate	7. accrue	8. upbeat		

B. Missing Words

1. prevalent	2. student	3. philosophers	4. little	5. regardless

C. Antonyms

1. unbiased	2. extol	3. honorable	4. ignorant	5. camouflage
6. crush	7. bogus	8. expand		

D. Idioms

1. d	2. g	3. a	4. f	5. c
6. b	7. e			

Set 47: Answers

A. Synonyms

1.storyteller	2. enemy	3. limber	4. plush	5. vivacity
6. falsehood	7. reveal	8. integrated		

B. Fill in the blanks

1. consternation	2. gradation	3. loveless	4. foolhardy	5. consecutive

C. Homographs

1. you'll	2. whoa	3. spirit	4. woe	5. yule
6. address	7. address	8. spirit		

D. Synonyms - Spelling

1. fitting	2. crazy	3. impressive	4. graceful	5. passage
6. effect	7. enroll			

Set 48: Answers

A. Synonyms

1. deceive	2. harmful	3. healthy	4. narcotic	5. expert
6. grasping	7. dreariness	8. wasted		

B. Missing Words

1. naturally	2. power	3. bandwagon	4. market	5. all round

C. Antonyms

1. independent	2. choice	3. perfection	4. peaceful	5. tardily
6. opulence	7. dolefully	8. inadvertently		

D. Idioms

1. g	2. a	3. b	4. c	5. d
6. e	7. f			

Set 49: Answers

A. Synonyms

1. wondrous	2. worn	3. renounce	4. anomaly	5. dwelling
6. wretched	7. cynic	8. ploy		

B. Fill in the blanks

1. irrevocably	2. immune	3. efface	4. scripture	5. dictate

C. Homographs

1. bag	2. raw	3. rebel	4. roar	5. world
6. bag	7. whirled	8. rebel		

D. Synonyms - Spelling

1. flora	2. unsettle	3. slang	4. grind	5. quagmire
6. remedy	7. acclaim			

Set 50: Answers

A. Synonyms

1. iota	2. dulcet	3. confident	4. maxim	5. furtive
6. fluency	7. reserved	8. brazen		

B. Missing Words

1. selection	2. proficient	3. forte	4. read	5. inclusive

C. Antonyms

1. contented	2. agitate	3. dismiss	4. affable	5. odorless
6. assimilate	7. retain	8. ignoramus		

D. Idioms

1. f	2. e	3. g	4. a	5. b
6. c	7. d			

Made in United States
Troutdale, OR
12/28/2023

16495079R00077